I0817625

HOW TO DISAPPEAR AND WHY

KYLE MINOR

ESSAYS

Sarabande Books · Louisville, Kentucky

Earlier versions of portions of this manuscript originally appeared in
New England Review, *New Ohio Review*, and
New York Times Book Review.

Publisher's Cataloging-in-Publication
(Provided by Cassidy Cataloguing Services, Inc.)
Names: Minor, Kyle, author.
Title: How to disappear and why : essays / Kyle Minor.
Description: First edition. | Louisville, Kentucky : Sarabande Books, [2026]
Identifiers: ISBN: 9781956046571 (paperback) | 9781956046588 (ebook)
Subjects: LCSH: Disappearances (Parapsychology) | Vanishings
(Parapsychology) | Ghosts. | Temples. | Exile
(Punishment) | LCGFT: Essays.
Classification: LCC: PS3613.I657 H68 2026 | DDC: 814/.6--dc2

All efforts to obtain permission from rightsholders have been made.
Cover by Danika Isdahl.
Printed in the USA on acid-free paper.
Sarabande Books is a nonprofit literary organization.

This project is supported in part by an award from the National Endowment
for the Arts. The Kentucky Arts Council, the state arts agency, supports
Sarabande Books with state tax dollars and federal funding
from the National Endowment for the Arts.

for Nia and Dylan

CONTENTS

How to Disappear and Why

I.
(THIRTEEN NOTIONS TO INTERROGATE)

Heavy pink-lined clouds to the north
tell me where land is, but I feel glad
not to see it just now.

—Bernard Moitessier

How to Disappear and Why

I. Reasons to Disappear

Perhaps you are ashamed.

Perhaps the Lord turned you for seven years into an animal like Nebuchadnezzar.

Perhaps you were ordered by a court to disappear into incarceration.

Perhaps you were ordered at gunpoint to disappear into exile.

Perhaps something in the culture has made you afraid.

Perhaps something in your secret life has made you afraid.

Perhaps like Handkerchief Moody the one you loved has rejected your love and you no longer want another to see your own face.

Perhaps your public success has activated the jealousy of others and you are afraid to continue to be seen.

Perhaps you have seen the public success of others activate the jealousy of people who desire what the others have, and although you have no evidence that your own small success, real or imagined, has activated the jealousy of people in your own circle, you are still afraid that too much ongoing exposure will activate such a jealousy, and therefore you are afraid to continue to be seen.

Perhaps your public success has activated the indignance of others because of something you said or did, or something you were perceived to have said or done, or something that you accidentally or intentionally represent, and which is now deemed to be foul, and you are afraid to continue to be seen.

Perhaps you have been threatened.

Perhaps you are tired of the sound of your own voice.

Perhaps you have been wounded by something someone else has said.

Perhaps you are tired of the derision of others/not being embraced by others.

Perhaps you are tired of the company of others.

Perhaps you want to purify the world by eradicating the self.

Perhaps your reasons for wanting to be known or seen have been satiated.

Perhaps your reasons for wanting to be known or seen have gone away.

Perhaps the one you were hoping to please with your performance has died.

Perhaps you have finally capitulated to your disappointment.

Perhaps you have changed your mind.

Perhaps you realized that your public position was very wrong, and you refused to try to cash in one more time by refuting yourself.

Perhaps your disappearance from public was involuntary, and you were unable to cause yourself to reappear despite your best efforts.

Perhaps you realized that your absence from the eyes of the world would make the mysterious idea of you more tantalizing.

Perhaps you realized that your continued presence before the eyes of the world would weary the world's eyes.

Perhaps you lost a dispute over money, walked away, and failed to realize that the money that only served your interest inadvertently was what was keeping you from disappearing.

Perhaps you committed suicide.

Perhaps you became committed to a consuming new pursuit, such as bowhunting or weeks-long meditation, that was incompatible with what being visible required.

Perhaps you wanted others to wonder where you went.

Perhaps you wanted no one to remember you had been.

Perhaps you could no longer bear the meager attentions of others in response to your vigorous bids for attention.

Perhaps you had a true desire to commune with nature.

Perhaps you had a true desire to commune with one and only one other person with whom you could disappear together.

II. Ways to Disappear

By boat.

By plane.

By train.

By legal name change.

By ditching your technology and going "off the grid."

By moving to an isolated island in the vast Pacific.

By becoming a wilderness guide in a remote place and telling no one.

By staying indoors in an upstairs room until they forget.

By dressing plainly and walking around discount stores at night.

By allowing yourself to grow old enough to become invisible to younger people.

By accepting your prison sentence.

By burning down your house and absconding with the insurance money.

By burning down your house and absconding without the insurance money.

By burning your face and cutting out your tongue.

By moving away quietly and telling no one you were leaving or where you were going.

By joining a monastic order.

By joining nothing, ever.

By rejecting the possibility of friendship.

By rejecting the possibility of love.

By rejecting shame and turning inward.

By embracing shame and turning inward.

By ceasing speech.

By ceasing the efforts of your typing hands.

By typing all you want, like J. D. Salinger, but ceasing to publish.

By renouncing public life.

By renouncing life altogether.

By acceding to your growing paranoia.

By easing your paranoia through a period of chill that gradually becomes the rest of your life.

By accepting and internalizing the persistent rejection from others.

III. What You Think They Will Say

What a relief that he is gone.

What a relief that she is gone.
How I wish that he had not gone.
How I wish that she had not gone.
Where did he go?
Where did she go?

IV. What They Will Say

Almost nothing, right away.
Almost nothing, after a while.
Almost nothing, ever.

V. Imaginaries to Disappear Into

The machine that stops time for everyone else but allows you to move freely through space, manipulating matter, setting things right for others.

The machine that stops time for everyone else but allows you to move freely through space, stealing whatever you want, destroying whatever's in your way, secretly reordering the world for the exclusive benefit of yourself and those you love.

The machine that enables you to drop adult consciousness into your infant brain, so you can do everything over in the way you now know would make everything better.

The device you put on your face that allows you to pretend that you are moving through a better or more interesting world than the one you actually inhabit.

Stories, movies, books.

VI. Stories, Movies, Books

> A story is not like a road to follow, I said. It's more like a house. You go inside and stay there for a while,

> wandering back and forth and settling where you like and discovering how the room and corridors relate to each other, how the world outside is altered by being viewed from these windows. And you, the visitor, the reader, are altered as well by being in this enclosed space, whether it is ample and easy or full of crooked turns, or sparsely or opulently furnished. You can go back again and again, and the house, the story, always contains more than you saw the last time. It has also a sturdy sense of itself, of being built out of its own necessity, not just to shelter or beguile you.
>
> —Alice Munro

VII. Real Things to Disappear Into

Manual labor.

Intellectual labor.

All-consuming family life.

Religious labor.

Ideology.

Military service (clerical).

Military service (food preparation).

Military service (rifles, battles, machinery, war).

Prayer or meditation.

Obsessive routines of exercise.

Obsessive collecting (vinyl records, stamps, toys, sports memorabilia, stuffed animals, autographs, automobiles, camera equipment, seashells, books, beer cans, antique furniture, shoes, dolls, models, musical instruments).

The obscurity of poverty.

The obscurity of ordinary public service.

The obscurity afforded by long retreat behind the high walls that can be bought by the not-squandered wages of previously monetized fame.

VIII. People Who Famously Disappeared

Amelia Earhart, whose airplane disappeared in 1937 somewhere in the Pacific, east of New Guinea, during an attempt to circumnavigate the globe.

Assata Shakur, who escaped the Clinton Correctional Facility for Women in 1979, where she was serving a life sentence for the murder of a New Jersey state trooper, and who is still subject, at age seventy-five, to a $2 million fugitive bounty as the only woman on the FBI Most Wanted Terrorists list.

Elizabeth Ann Duke, who jumped bail in 1985 after indictment for her role in the United States Capitol bombing, and who is still subject, at age eighty-two, to a $50,000 fugitive bounty by the FBI.

Bill Knott, who wrote a letter published in a 1966 issue of the literary journal *Epoch*, which said that Bill Knott, age twenty-six, had killed himself in a tenement room on North Clark Street in Chicago, and that his body was on its way to Michigan to be buried, then published his first volume of poems under the pseudonym Saint Geraud (1940–1966), although he would not die for another forty-eight years.

IX. People Who Famously Were Disappeared

Edward V, uncrowned child king of England, who was locked in the Tower of London in 1483 by his uncle, the future King Richard III, and who was never seen again.

Solomon Northup, a Black violinist from New York who was drugged and kidnapped in Washington, DC, in 1841, and sold into twelve years of slavery on a Louisiana plantation.

Aleksandr Solzhenitsyn, who joined the Red Army, denounced Stalin, spent eight years at forced labor in the Gulag, found himself sentenced to exile-for-life in Kazakhstan, wrote the authoritative history of his repressive government's network of political prison labor camps, enjoyed a brief reprieve from Khrushchev, fell out of favor again when Khrushchev died, lost his citizenship, was declared a nonperson, won a Nobel Prize for Literature he was forbidden from traveling to Sweden to collect, fled to unfashionable exile in America . . .

X. Why You Are Not Famous

There are eight billion people in the world.

There are 1.5 million new books published each year.

There are over 80 million songs available for streaming.

There are 500,000 feature-length movies currently in existence, if not all in circulation.

There are 195 countries in the world today.

You are not quite smart enough.

You are smart enough, but so is the competition, and there are a lot of them.

You are too smart to fit the most promising category.

You are in the wrong body.

You are in the right body, but you don't want to use it in that certain way.

You are in the wrong body, but you have so far been unwilling to do the things you have to do to make it the right body.

You were born into the wrong family.

You were born into the right family, but you were the wrong child.

You were born into the right family, and you were the right child, but you had the wrong desires.

You were born into the right family, and you were the right child, and you had the right desires, but something changed at just the wrong time.

Your father is not a famous actor, writer, director, athlete, or pop star.

Your mother is not a famous actor, writer, director, athlete, or pop star.

Unlike the father and mother of Taylor Swift, neither your father nor your mother has the money and/or the will to move your family to Nashville, finance your demos, buy a stake in your record label, make a call to . . .

Even if your father or mother had the money and the will, you are not Taylor Swift.

There are certain sacrifices you have so far been unable to make.

There are certain sacrifices you have been willing to make, at great cost to yourself and others, but it didn't work out the way you imagined it might.

You never quite had a shot.

You had a shot, but you didn't take it.

You had a shot, and you tried to take it, but it came too early, and you weren't properly prepared.

You had a shot, and you tried to take it, but someone darkly intervened.

You had a shot, and you tried to take it, but you missed.

You had more than one shot, and you blew it more than once.

You had a shot, and you took it, and it was glorious, but it came at the wrong time, so it didn't work out the way you would have imagined it might.

You had a shot, and you took it, and it was glorious, and it came at the right time, but you were in the wrong body, so it didn't work out the way you would have imagined it might.

You had a shot, and you took it, and it was glorious, and it came at the right time, and you were in the right body, but it still didn't work out the way you would have imagined it might.

You have not yet had the opportunity to take a shot, so you don't yet know if it will work out in the way you imagine it might.

You have not yet properly prepared to take the shot you may or may not have the opportunity to take.

You have not yet properly narrativized the advantages that greeted you at birth.

You have not yet properly publicized the narrativization of the advantages that greeted you at birth.

You have not yet properly monetized the narrativization of the advantages that greeted you at birth.

You have not yet properly narrativized your tragedies.

You have not yet properly publicized your tragedies.

You have not yet properly monetized your tragedies.

XI. Why No One Should Want to Be Famous

It separates you from other people in an unnatural way.

It causes others to be unable to relate to you in a natural way.

It insulates you from understanding how the world generally works.

It causes you to be isolated from others out of self-protective necessity.

It causes you to inadvertently leak all your previously secret pathologies into the realm of public knowledge.

It doesn't scratch the actual itch you meant it to scratch.

It puts a big fucking bullseye on your chest.

XII. Of All the Reasons to Disappear, the Worst Reason to Disappear

> Take the simple case of the sarge who can't go back
> to war
> 'Cause the hippies tore down everything that he was
> fighting for.
>
> —Neil Young

XIII. Of All the Reasons to Disappear, the Best Reasons to Disappear

Perhaps you need to tend to the health of a loved one.

Perhaps you need to tend to your own health.

Perhaps you are unable to tend your own health, you know that soon you will die, and while you still can on your own terms, you withdraw from public life.

Perhaps you are a famous film actor, or a former president, or the Queen of England, and you're keenly aware of dementia's steady progress, and while you still can on your own terms, you withdraw from public life.

Perhaps you are less than keenly aware of dementia's steady progress, but you take your spouse at her or his word, and withdraw from public life.

Perhaps you see the war coming and you must flee.

Perhaps you see the draft coming and you must either join the war or flee.

Perhaps the war is over and you see what the new peace will be and it is ominous and you must flee.

Perhaps it's clear the war will never be over and you must flee to a place where there will not always be war.

Perhaps you just won three hundred million dollars in the lottery and you need a little separation so you can keep yourself safe.

Perhaps you are in the presence of a wild animal and you need a little distance so you can keep yourself safe.

Perhaps you are in the presence of a skilled professional and you need a little distance so you can keep yourself safe.

Perhaps you are in the presence of yourself in the presence of something or someone you can no longer abide and you need a little space so you can keep yourself alive.

Perhaps you want to give others a little space to say what they need to say.

Perhaps you need time to sort out what you need to say.

Perhaps you've said all you need to say.

Perhaps you have nothing left to say.

II.
(THREE GHOSTS OF PERSONAL PREOCCUPATION)

Yet on the walls of my brain, frescoes . . .

—William Goyen

A Theory of Ghosts

I had come to believe—with no good justification—that ghosts, like the particles of quantum foam, like God, exist outside of time.

Because you began speaking to me before you were dead.

Because you spoke in two voices.

First, the voice of the man, alive, carrying that shabby coffee cup, asking for rides to the grocery store, getting in fights at the bar.

Then—so ungently—the voice of the ghost, no less alive for speaking from outside time.

No less alive for being dead.

*

Who were you when you were alive?

~~You refused to drive a car to the grocery store because you did not want to contribute to~~

~~The coffee cup was shabby because Styrofoam was not built for hundreds of uses and you did not want to contribute to~~

I do not believe in war, you said, *but absolutely I will fight any motherfucker who . . .*

*

That night your one eye was half closed because you did not fight back.

That night there is no doubt you picked the fight.

~~The frat boy was so angry~~

Twice you'd made him so angry. First when you wanted the fight. Then when you wouldn't punch him back.

The photojournalist's job is to run toward the bullets, your ghost says. *It's the same with literature. It's the same with friendship.*

When I ran to the fight, the frat boy's animal teeth wet eyes bruised knuckles howl of animal rage. *Hit me. Why won't you hit me?*

*

That night we went to the ATM machine.

Half, you said. *You pay the other half that's your fault.*

The tow truck driver raised the wrench at your approach.

Not the drunk redneck, he said. *The little clean guy.*

~~Before I paid him, you~~

Your two steps forward. The eight words you said.

Swing it if you want.

I'm dead already.

*

That night you were hungry.

At the all-night place you pulled at your collar.

Look at my neck, you said. *It* is *red.*

You pulled at your shirtsleeves.

The skin dotted with pink scars.

Mementos, you said. *My mother liked to put out her cigarettes on me.*

*

~~*This is who I am,* the ghost said.~~

*

That night I wanted to argue with the ghost.

Tonight I want to argue with myself about the ghost.

To say:

He spoke six languages fluently.

He was passionate about ranked-choice voting.

He wrote a doctoral dissertation on how existentialism might speak into the aftermath of atrocity and trauma.

He introduced me to the works of Solzhenitsyn, Dostoyevsky, Chekhov, Brecht, Wisława Szymborska.

Pseudonymously he wrote many books, some alone, some in collaboration with others. Less often he used his own name. Science fiction epics. Political biographies. Collections of poetry and short fiction.

Pseudonymously he self-published a series of teenage vampire romance novels.

That night, you said:

Better to be a ghost than a vampire.

Can you imagine how terrible it would be to live forever?

*

That night you stood on a chair and made an announcement.

I am a bisexual.

No one in the all-night place put down her or his burrito.

No one turned head fixed eyes inclined ears.

~~No one~~

I want, you said, *to give you a blowjob. Don't worry. It won't mean anything. Nothing means anything.*

(*Everything means,* I say now to the ghost, *everything.*)

*

> A starving child is a frightful sight. A starving vampire, even worse.
>
> —Anne Rice

*

Never mind, you said. *I'm not going to give you a blowjob.*

Not because you seem afraid.

Not because you're so hetero.

Because I know you.

You can't separate the heart from the body.

For you the act is bound up in love.

*

That night we walked you home beside the Olentangy River.

A soft rain fell on the water heavy from last night's hard rain.

All that water plus the sewage overflow.

You sniffed the ~~fragrant~~ fetid air.

1974, you drunkenly said. *Lightning at the Pennwalt Chemical Building. Explosion, fires. The big spill. Four miles of dead fish.*

The sound you made.

Like the deathcry of four miles of fish.

The rattle of your Sasquatch burp.

*

That night I talked you out of the cigarettes, the twenty-four-pack of Pabst Blue Ribbon, the liquor store.

That night you wrote a poem about eating grease.

That night you said please don't leave me alone with the thoughts all in me.

That night you told me for the first time how your father met your mother.

*

She—your mother—was the nineteen-year-old secretary at the

construction site trailer.

He was—sixty-five? Seventy?—old enough to be her grandfather.

(I ask the ghost if I rightly remember the details, but the ghost gives no answer.)

She had deficits, you said.

Occasionally she defecated in the corner of the living room, behind her chair.

Did your teenage sisters petition the court for emancipation? Is that how they took you into their custody? Or did they just leave the state with you and nobody gave chase?

Saints and heroes, you said. *Girls. They raised me like they were women.*

Helped the boy through high school, college, study abroad stints in Germany, Poland, Mexico, and Quebec, graduate study in literature, creative writing, philosophy, and law.

Out of Kentucky.

Into North Carolina and the world.

Out of poverty.

Into something that was starting to seem sustainable.

*

That night you said the most important people in the world were librarians.

I went to the bathroom. When I came out you were gone. When the front door opened, it was:

You.

An unlit cigarette dangling between your lips.

A bottle of Jack Daniel's.

A twenty-four-pack of Pabst Blue Ribbon.

Let's read books, you said.

A weird fire in your eyes.

A mad dash to the bedroom.

I heard a rustling sound.

You came back with paper bags full of books.

You made three trips.

I don't want to talk about my mother, you said.

You dumped the books all over the floor. About each one there was something to say. A line, a form, a voice, a structure. Jerzy Kosinski, Richard Wright, Samuel Beckett, Simone de Beauvoir, Jean-Paul Sartre, Charles Wright, Slavoj Žižek, C. D. Wright, Yukio Mishima, Joyce Carol Oates, José Saramago, Franz Wright, Terrance Hayes . . .

You held up a copy of Frank Stanford's *The Battlefield Where the Moon Says I Love You. 15,283 lines,* you said, *by a boy adopted from the home for unwed mothers. 383 pages by the boy raised on the levees of the Mississippi. The boy who said,* Oh Sweet Jesus the levees that break in my heart.

You held up a copy of Forrest Gander's *As a Friend. A love letter,* you said, *to Frank Stanford. He hangs a horse skull from the ceiling for his lover C. D. Wright. He fills it with gasoline. He throws a match. The skull breathes fire from its nostrils.*

You said:

Satan, bring me my guitar.

What if all the flowers in the world were petrified?

What if the ferryman of Hades had three lanterns?

You lifted your black T-shirt and scratched your round belly.

Manic, and growing more manic, you held up a copy of Aleksandr Solzhenitsyn's *One Day in the Life of Ivan Denisovich* and read the ending: *There were three thousand six hundred and fifty-three days in his sentence, from reveille to lights out. The three extra days were because of the leap years.*

*

Later you said that was the night.

Something broke in me that night.

Before that night you said you might be falling in love with the nurse.

After that night you called from Montreal to say you were smoking crack in a hotel room with some homeless people you met on the street outside the window.

It got better, then it got worse.

The ghost the night she he we perceived the pattern.

Betterworse betterworse betterworsebetter.

*

The solution was Roman Catholicism. Before that, the right job at the right university. Before that, existentialism and atrocity studies. Before that, the online certificate in legal investigation, the one-act plays, the small press cooperative, the trips to Mexico City, the trip to Russia.

Always, the late-night phone calls:

Achievement Unlocked: Presidential Fellowship.

Achievement Unlocked: The Harvard Review.

Achievement Unlocked: A Note from Joyce Carol Oates.

Achievement Unlocked: Permission for the translations from the German publisher.

Achievement Unlocked: I met this woman from Poland . . .

Achievement Unlocked: I met this woman from France . . .

Achievement Unlocked: I have learned the Pho-sho secret of bone broth . . .

Achievement Unlocked: As of today I am 20 percent fluent in Korean.

Achievement Unlocked: As of today, I can get around in seven Romance languages and dialects.

Achievement Unlocked: As of today, I have at least once hobo-surfed the roof of a moving city bus.

Achievement Unlocked: As of today, there are only three concepts in calculus I have not mastered . . .

Achievement Not Unlocked: There are quarks inside the protons, and gluons between the quarks, but there is a big empty space inside me, Kyle, a vast nothing, a vacuum, a void, I mean it, nothing will fill it, it's pointless, a big fucking hole, it's never going away.

*

A phone call from the hospital. Collect. Will you accept the charges?

You were laid up in a white room.

Later you sent a photograph.

Tubes in your nose. Tubes in your arms. Cuts on your face. Bruises. A thumbs-up from a traction sling. A weird smile. *I'll have scars,* you said. *Free tattoos.*

Two men jumped you outside a liquor store. Did they want money?

You quoted perversely from a poem:

I took it.

It wasn't the money I needed.

But I took it.

Your laughter turned. A dark joke became a thick cough. *That sure as fuck hurt every organ,* you said. *My body's saying sleep a little now. Maybe sleep it off forever.*

That talk. Four alarms in my firehouse. Was it the ghost speaking or the opiates in the vein drip?

A phone call from convalescence in your Pennsylvania apartment. *A wicked thing, amigo. I never ask about your children. What tribe have they chosen? Have they taken to ghost stories, kung fu movies, Ninja Turtles?*

*

Before I gave it, I knew my answer was an answer you'd love.

Mythical Japanese battling monsters who could be scooped up and contained in magical balls.

Their taxonomy was enormous enough to fill volumes as large as phone books.

Their backstories—which my children could recite in great detail—were drenched in great sadness:

Charmander, the dinosaur who must forever tend the flame that burns at the tip of its tail, because he will die if it is extinguished.

Banette, the doll that was thrown away and now wanders the earth searching for the child who discarded it.

Nosepass, who can never achieve face-to-face intimacy with another of his species because their magnetic noses, being of the same polarity, violently repel each other.

Absol, the disaster Pokémon, who makes the long journey down from his mountaintop to warn people before disaster arrives, only to find that he becomes a convenient object of blame for the disaster that follows his arrival, and who I have come to regard as the closest thing to a patron saint the secular world has delivered unto me.

What's the saddest? you said. *Tell me the saddest.*

The saddest—the Yamask—arose from the spirits of children whose bodies lay decaying in graves. These spirits, I told you, retain the child's memories. Life, love, and loss. At night the Yamask wanders the ruins of its childhood town, wearing a flesh mask that had once been its face when it was still alive.

*

It would be a Catholic funeral.

A seventeen-hour drive with my two young sons.

You were distant from me in other ways. Tethered by cellular service to the interior lives of others—all the weasel platforms of the internet—I tried to reconcile the conflicting stories as I drove:

He died young. He was a middle-aged white man.

He was an avatar of his poverty. He abused his high privilege. He inspired women and men. He was terrible to men. He was terrible to women.

I am conflicted about this inspiring terrible man. I am sad that he died. It is a triumph that he died.

He had diabetes. His heart gave out. He died in his sleep. He died in peace. He died in pain. He died on purpose. He died of sadness. His life was an overcoming triumph. He died as he had lived, an avatar of shame. He hadn't survived the bout of septic shock, after all.

Secretly he was an alcoholic. Publicly and belligerently he was an alcoholic.

He had dialed back the alcohol in service to a vision of Christ. He had used the idea of Christ to paper over his public sins.

To escape accountability.

He had always been a person trouble found, the ghost said, composing his own eulogy, *except that sometimes he found the trouble before the trouble found him.*

If you were dead, why could I hear your voice so clearly as I was driving?

We left in the dark and arrived in the Pennsylvania light.

*

The light here, you once wrote, *is a light I could live in if I came to terms with certain failings in my character and the character of others.*

*

The Catholics who presided over the eulogy spoke of your annoying convert's zeal.

Your long lists of theological, historical, and philosophical questions that the lay teachers of the rite of reception in the order of the Catechumenate could not easily answer.

Your long memorized portions of the catechetical texts.

Your overcommitment to the minutiae of the rite of Election, the period of reflection, purification, and enlightenment, and the Scrutiny rituals of self-examination and reflection.

Your recent enrollment, as a layperson, in graduate-level seminary courses.

Your refusal to buy a car. Not even a cheap Buick beater.

Your willingness to destroy the environment with the exhaust fumes of the cars of others but not your own.

Your unwillingness to use more than one Styrofoam coffee cup per year.

The disgustingness of your shabby coffee cup.

Your mismatched clothes.

I preferred the family recently immigrated from Thailand who ran the restaurant where we joined several of the other out-of-town guests for dinner.

I preferred the family member who stopped by our table to ask who we were and why we were in town.

When we said it was you, your funeral, she dignified our grief with her own. *Wait,* she said. She went into the kitchen, and returned with a picture. *Is this your friend?*

Yes.

One involuntary tear made a line on her cheek. *Oh, no,* she said. She went back into the kitchen. We heard the banging of pots and pans. Crying.

A man in a chef's hat appeared at our table. *He ate here almost every day,* he said. *He tried to learn our language. He talked so much. His Thai was so bad.*

*

For five years I've been working on this letter to you—in Indiana, in Nashville, in New Mexico and California, in Hiroshima—and I can't do better than the chef.

My plans were grand, literary.

Ghosts, and their reasons for going away and not going away. *Beloved*, Henry James, Shakespeare, *The Sixth Sense*, *Hamlet*, the headless horseman, the *chimères* of Haiti's Cité Soleil, *Brigadoon*, *Shoeless Joe*, Abraham Lincoln emerging from Winston Churchill's bathtub, the White Lady, the Grey Lady, the hungry ghosts of the Hua-yen Sutra, the werebeast forms of the Filipino aswang, the possessing dybbuk, the Ghost of Christmas Past.

That's the kind of fancy stuff I wanted.

I went to the university library where you worked on your dissertation. Pulled the books I knew you'd touched. Solzhenitsyn. Dostoyevsky. Husserl. Hannah Arendt.

Pencil marks in the margins. Notes.

Yours.

~~Notes from the ghost.~~

~~For me it was too much~~

Too much hurt. Too much feeling.

I closed the books. I left the library.

*

Tonight I'm thinking of the Old Testament prophets. Jeremiah, thrown into a cistern, sinking into the mud. Elijah, taken up to heaven in a chariot of fire. Jonah thrown overboard in a storm, swallowed by the whale, vomited onto the beach, pouting under a sheltering vine until its root is eaten by the worm.

*

I have come to believe—as you believed—that ghosts do not live forever.

When I returned to the library not all of the books were gone. Not all of the notes were gone.

~~Your hand your scrawl your~~

Someone had erased ~~your annotations your pencil marks you're—~~

You

—from Husserl, from Hannah Arendt.

~~Not all of you was gone~~

~~You were gone.~~

All of you is gone.

You were my friend.

An acquaintance to beauty. No stranger to ugliness. Flawed, wounded, a fountain of generosity, a bringer of harm.

I loved you. I didn't want you to disappear.

The Uber Diaries

Indianapolis, Indiana. Somewhere near Keystone Avenue and 62nd Street my iPhone pings. A college student from Hyderabad, India. He is pleased when I tell him he's my first customer. He tips me two dollars.

*

I pick up my second customer in front of a bar in Broad Ripple. He gets in the front seat. His hair is grown to thigh length, and he is on some kind of party drug that makes him want to touch things.

"Please stop rubbing my arm," I say.

He apologizes.

Near Rocky Ripple, he takes off his shoes and socks and rubs his bare feet on the windshield.

His feet leave little rabbit marks. He is a large man with very tiny feet. When I drop him off at the donut shop, he doesn't leave a tip.

*

Dusk, a half mile from the bars on Massachusetts Avenue, stuck behind a long train. The man is silent, but the woman is chatty.

"What made you become a rideshare driver?" she says.

"Money," I say.

"Do you have a day job?" she says.

"I teach, but not in the summer."

"You need to learn to manage your money better," the man says. Now he talks. "I bet you think about that a lot, driving people around in your car."

The train cars keep coming. No caboose in sight.

"Why didn't you save your money?" the man says.

"It's a long story," I say.

"We've got time."

I tell him everything. The book I wrote. The big promises from the movie people in California last summer. The Nazi submarines off the coast of Alabama. The long commutes. The office on the studio lot where they used to shoot *Gilligan's Island* and *Seinfeld*. The famous producer who stood me up in Silver Lake. The famous producer who stood me up in Ojai. The propaganda documentary for the Hillary Clinton campaign. The dustup about Meryl Streep. The elderly lady in Iowa. The nights I slept on the floor of the abandoned fitness center in Encino. The place with the saltwater pool in Santa Clarita. The flophouse in Santa Ana. The credit cards. The check that never arrived.

"You know what?" the man says. "It sounds like you're lying."

Mercifully, the final cars of the train. Mercifully, the caboose.

"You know what?" the man says. "You're a terrible liar."

*

The pings come slowly between nine and ten thirty, but at eleven o'clock the heat map turns colors, and every fare comes with a multiplier. 1.3x, 1.7x, 2x. Surge Time. In the money time.

Two quick rides, nice drunks. The neighborhood bar to the house around the corner. Then a car full of teenagers complaining about love. Two married lovers holding hands, calling the babysitter on the cell phone.

Then trouble.

Four people, two men, two women, on Guilford Road, standing outside a giant white concrete hair comb that pulls double duty as club logo and security barrier. The guy who gets in first says thanks for picking us up, but the guy who got in second comes in yelling: "Let's get the show on the road, you asshole."

He must think it is funny to call me "you asshole," because he keeps saying it. None of the other people laugh. He asks the other couple how often they have sex. "You're husband and wife," he says. "Three times a day, three times a week, three times a month?"

The other guy keeps saying, "Shut up, man." I look in the rearview mirror. The woman sitting beside him has fallen asleep. "We got to get her home," the other guy says. There is an argument about how to get her home. She lives a half hour north, in Carmel, but everyone else wants to drink some more a few blocks south, near 54th Street.

They're still arguing when we reach the bar. The woman wakes up. "I'll pay you cash to take her home," her husband says. At that moment she makes an ungodly noise. "Oh, god, don't throw up in the car," the mean guy says. She vomits all over the seat, all over the floor. Wet flecks of white land on my arm and the dash. The car smells like alcohol and fish tacos, plus the requisite stomach acid.

"What's the cleaning fee?" the mean guy says.

I say two hundred dollars, but I don't know. It's my first night.

"Make it right," the other guy says. "Make it right."

"What if I give you one hundred and we call it even," the mean guy says. "It's not even my wife, it's his, see how nice I am?" He's standing over me, using his larger body to intimidate me. "Here." He shoves a wad of cash into my pocket.

OK, I say, but it's not OK. There's anger in the air, the parking lot is mostly empty, it's dark, and I am afraid.

At home, after blotting the puke, sprinkling the baking soda, shampooing the carpet, scrubbing the stain with liquid cleanser and a toothbrush, I remember to check my pocket, count the cash. Twenty-five dollars.

At the convenience store I buy some air freshener and spray it around and head back to the bar district. What else is there to do? I've already lost an hour and a half of Surge Time.

*

The next afternoon, a gated apartment complex off 78th Street, and the gate will not open. I call the rider. "I can't give you the code," she says. I ask if she can walk toward the gate and open it. "Wait for another car to open it," she says, "then follow them in."

A little later, a guy in an apartment complex. "Do you like chess?" he says. "I just played six games of chess and lost every game." I ask him what he does for a living. "I have a degree in urban planning," he says, "but right now I'm doing IT for a used car lot." I ask if he's happy. "No," he says. "I want to make cities."

A couple days later a morning ping. Butler University campus, next to the Hinkle Fieldhouse where the basketball miracles happen. A twenty-seven-year-old woman on her way to Georgia to pick up her technology and design MFA at the Savannah College of Art and Design. "You're early," she's saying. "You're hustling. I like that." I ask her what's next. Is she looking for a job in Indianapolis or Georgia?

"Oh, I already have a job," she says. "A San Francisco tech company. I had other offers. They had to fight for me. A great CEO. Already he's my buddy, my friend. Stock options that vest in five years. I own my IP. Do you know IP? It stands for intellectual property. A lot of people my age haven't made such smart choices as I have. They don't have a brand. I have a brand. I own my own products. That's why I have so much leverage with my new company."

A soft rain begins to fall.

"I hate this weather," she says. "Donald Trump is the cause of climate change, you know it? I mean, not really, but it's fun to blame him for everything. He's terrible. What a clusterfuck. I mean, I'm a Republican but we need universal health care. But it's not fair to be shitty to rich people. I plan to be rich people. You see those Asian kids, they're driving those $90,000 cars? You probably think they don't deserve it. But here's what people forget. Wherever there's money, there's someone, somewhere in the past, who busted his ass to get it. Someone in the family. People forget that. That's the American dream, right? I mean, I'm young, I get it, but most people don't get it. It's there. You just have to go get it. You have to go out there and take it."

At the airport she takes my shoulders in her hands and tells me again: You have to go out there and take it.

*

Sometimes when I get home from driving, at night or after daylight, I feel wound up, adrenalized, like I used to feel after I played a rock show with my college band. In the internet's dark corners other drivers share advice, complaints, tips for maximizing my money.

I read the message boards. I watch the violent videos. The taxi drivers in Johannesburg, South Africa, setting the Uber cars on fire. The inebriated medical doctor in Miami who swings at her driver, smashes his iPhone, and breaks his rearview mirror, because he won't give her a ride. The racist NYPD traffic cop who berates the immigrant driver and punches his car for honking at the unmarked police car that parallel parked without using a blinker. The Uber SUV that goes airborne, jumps a curb, barrels through a parking lot, crashes through a gas pump at a Shell station in Seattle, sets off an explosion.

The other drivers say Uber has secret spy software. Everything has a code name. The "Godview" program can see into your car at any time. The "Hell" program tracks drivers on competitor platforms like Lyft. The "Grayball" program routes drivers away from local police.

A consensus is hardening. Best practices. Don't chase the Surge. Let the Surge come to you. Run two rideshare apps at all times, and don't be afraid to game them to get the highest fares, because that's what the customers do. There's more money in a five-minute wait-and-cancel than a ride down the street. Ignore all pings more than four minutes away. The app will penalize you for cancellations but not for ignoring pings. If you get called to a grocery store, cancel. They'll make you carry the groceries up four flights of stairs and they'll never tip. The money's in the distance, not the fare time. If someone asks you to go through the drive-thru, say no, unless it's a slow time, then ask them to buy you some food to compensate for your lost distance. If you don't like someone's face, if you feel fear, drive away, leave them at the curb. Ride share is a free market, supply and demand, and if you don't take advantage of the customer, the customer will take advantage of you. Grab all the control you can, then let go the illusion you have any control.

The app is your oracle. It predicts and determines your future.

*

I pick up Brian at the Pony, a strip club on Lafayette, the West Side. He seems to be about my age. A big guy. He wears a suit. He looks like a bank vice president. He reeks of alcohol. When I arrive, he opens the rear passenger door, throws his body down on my back seat, curls his feet up, begins snoring. I walk around to the other side of the car and close the door. I follow the app's directions to the address he's requested. He sleeps all the way to Zionsville, a twenty-minute drive. His house is palatial. When I pull into his driveway and stop the car, he wakes up, sits up, says thank you, opens his garage door, goes inside.

I look in the back seat to see what kind of mess he's made, but all I find is a five dollar bill he's tucked partway between the seat cushions.

*

At midnight I'm thinking three things:

1. I need to find a safe bathroom, badly.
2. This time two years ago, I was finishing a thirty-city book tour.
3. There is a Barry Hannah story titled "Midnight and I'm Not Famous Yet."

*

Another ping to the Pony. This time a woman in a black skirt. She says she's not a dancer, she's a stripper. She said another stripper showed her a funny thing on Twitter. She has a screenshot on her phone. She reads it to me:

"If you get a lap dance, remember: There's a thin layer of flesh and cartilage between you and a gyrating skeleton full of turds."

*

Night turns again to day, and I'm still driving. I pick up Marlon on 17th Street. He's going to work. He is a supervisor. "I make chicken sandwiches, egg-salad sandwiches," he says. "Anything you get at a gas station. Those are my sandwiches."

He says his mom is an Uber driver in Chicago. She makes $1,400 a week, more than double what I'm making. "You should talk to my mom," he says. He gives me her phone number. "I love my mom," he says. "I work in the cold. I'm so glad she doesn't work in the cold. I work in the freezer. I have to wear this jacket all the time, even when it's eighty degrees outside. I smell so bad sometimes. Can you smell me right now? I made this German chocolate cake. It only took a little while. There's a birthday girl at work."

I tell him about a bad thing that happened to me a few weeks ago. I was driving around at night, not working, listening to a podcast, when somebody I don't see shoots at my car. One through the back seat, one in the door. A Glock 9mm, the policeman said. Five hundred dollars to fix the damage. I feel lucky to be alive.

Marlon says he's so sorry. "You can't trust people anymore," he says. "My sister got shot at, in Wisconsin. Nine bullets. Her kids in the car. She was just sitting in the driveway and this face just popped up. Bang bang bang bang bang. Nine bullets in her body, point blank. None of them hit any of her vital organs. Can you believe it? It's a miracle. She survived."

We get to the entrance to the factory, and there is a line of taxis and Ubers outside the gate, letting people out so they can go to work. "Nobody has a car?" I say. "Oh, I see," Marlon says. "You're from a world where everyone has a car."

*

A lot of drunks lately.

Two in the morning, I pick up Luis outside a late-night bar downtown. He cries in the back seat all the way home.

I pick up Patrice at a dance club near the stadium. She slurs her words. "I majored in animal science," she says. "I know people who majored in accounting, law. You know about these people? They teach them a secret language so they can take from other people. They hurt other people. That's their job."

I pick up Natalie at the same club an hour later. "Will you drive me through Taco Bell?" she says. "I'll buy you anything you want." I'm hungry. I say yes. In her driveway we share eleven soft tacos, two burritos, and two Mountain Dew Baja Blast Freezes.

Such a sad night. Rain. The smell of alcohol coming out of mouths and pores. The smell of sadness. Rain and the smell of sadness.

I pick up Jeannine from a nightclub in Fountain Square. She asks me my favorite actress. "Sarah Paulson or maybe Maggie Gyllenhaal," I say. She asks me what I think about the Washington Redskins. "Good team, poorly named," I say. "Good answer," she says. "Did you go to college? You seem like someone who should have gone to college."

There is a particular pickled smell that rises from the skin of certain drinkers and lingers after they leave the car. I wonder if that smell has ever been on me. I vow to never drink again.

*

A passenger turns the radio to a Christian rock station. A woman sings: One day you're born, the next day you're dead.

*

Six in the morning. 56th Street. It's dark. I see a flashlight coming out from the house. A white man and a black woman. He says, "Hi, I'm Russell. This is my girlfriend, Wanda. Take good care of her, please."

Wanda is wearing a pink robe. She gets in the car. "On my way to chemo," she says. "Hang on." She lights up a cigarette. Usually I don't let people smoke in the car, but she is a cancer patient.

She opens her purse, and the whole car smells immediately of marijuana. "Sorry about that," she says. "CBD shrinks the tumor." She hands me eighteen weed-smelling dollars. "Just turn off the meter," she says. "It's on Russell's account, and I don't want him to have to pay every time I get chemo."

She pulls off her pink hoodie, then she pulls off the skullcap underneath it. Her head is bald. "Will you look at me for a minute?" she says. "I used to be so pretty. I wish you could've seen me. You would've loved me."

*

Outside a cowboy bar, I pick up a man in a cowboy hat. We ride in silence.

Somewhere near Speedway, he says, "You know what you should do? You should get a picture of a sick child and put it on your dashboard and tell people it's your own son sick with leukemia so you can get the big tips. People would feel so bad for you."

On 17th Street, near the fast-food place where the Indy 500 drivers got robbed at gunpoint, I pick up a home care nurse who weighs nearly four hundred pounds. She is sweating and panting. I open the front door, but she wants to sit in the back. "Move this seat up," she says. I ask if she wants me to adjust the air. "No," she says. She rolls the window down. "I'll do it this way, myself. I have to do it this way. I have my seasons."

At the airport, I wait in the taxi lot for my number to be called from the Uber queue. In the car next to me, I see another driver, a woman who looks to be in her late sixties or early seventies. Her seat is reclined and she's napping. The windows are going a little foggy. I see her phone is pinging, but she isn't answering. As best I can tell she is breathing.

When her phone stops pinging, mine starts. I've stolen her ride. It's a salesman in the steel fabrication business, flying in from Pittsburgh. He tells me about Chinese freighters, axle-welding robots, repurposed beams from skyscrapers. He asks how long I plan to keep driving, and I say September.

"Do you like movies?" he says. "Westerns?"

I say I do.

"You know how they end? The good ones? You've got a bunch of guys sitting around on horseback, and into the frame drives the Stanley steamer. Or you've got a bunch of cowboys firing their rifles, and someone wheels in a Gatling gun. That's what's about to happen to you. Have you heard about these self-driving cars?"

*

August begins but then it seems August will never end. I feel full up with the trouble of other people, but just when I make my peace with it, there's more.

Around one in the morning, I get a ping from a high school kid at Papa John's. He says he's been slinging pizzas since five o'clock. He says they were real backed up. A two-hour wait for delivery right now. I ask him why he didn't drive delivery. "First," he says, "I don't have a car. Second, my friend had a car, but he took it to a bad neighborhood and these guys stole it and burned it to the ground. Papa John's doesn't pay for that shit. You got to pay for your own car. Every time I think about that, I think: I hope he had insurance."

I pick up a heavily tattooed guy outside of Kilroy's in Broad Ripple. He is upset and mumbling. He keeps texting a woman. He says, "My girlfriend left me tonight at the bar. She was a stripper. I don't care that she goes on dates with other guys. Everyone has to make a living. The problem is: Are you religious? This girl, she's religious. This is what we always fight about. I hate it when she's religious. I'm judgmental about it. I'm hardly judgmental about anything, but I have to be judgmental about this. That shit isn't real! I've been arrested three times because of this girl. I went to jail one time already because of this girl. Hang on, she's texting me."

Kilroy's again. A woman named Kelsey. She has a guy with her. They get in the back seat. In a full voice, he tells her he thinks the driver is creepy and weird. They start making out. I hear his pants unzip. I'm not sure if she's giving him a blowjob, but I can tell that her cheek is at the very least resting against a part of the seat from which I've more than once sopped up vomit. When we reach their destination, she spits on the ground outside the car. Already they've started fighting about something. I hear their voices yelling as I drive away.

The Red Room, Broad Ripple. When I get there, a cop waves me over. He points to a woman slumped in a chair. "Can you get her to her door?" he says. I ask what's wrong. "She's near incoherent, she's very inebriated, and she wants to drive her car." He puts her in the back seat. She says, "I need to get my keys. Take me to get my keys." I roll down the window and ask the cop what I should do. He leans into the car and raises his voice at her. "Listen clearly," he says. "Understand me. If you get out of the car, you're going to jail. Do you understand?" Yes, she says. We drive. A block from the Red Room, she says, "I know where my car keys are. They're in my car, and the door is unlocked. Take me there." I tell her she can either get out of the car or let me take her home. We're in the only safe place for miles. She argues, then decides to get out. As she slams the door, she says, "You're the worst."

The Red Room again. Tommy. He's sitting in the back of a pickup truck with another big guy. "Let me finish this beer," he says. He slams it, throws it in a trash can, gets in the car. "Can you take me to the store? I need to buy cigarettes. I'll buy you something. What do you want?" A Coke, I say. On the way to the store, he tells me he's from Los Angeles. He was a firefighter. A smoke jumper. "You gave that up?" I say. He says he dropped out of a helicopter, and the rope broke when he was fifty feet from the ground. "I dropped straight down into the fire and broke my knee."

At the convenience store, he gets his cigarettes and I get my Coke and we take them to the front counter. He pats his shirt pocket, his pants pockets, his back pocket. "Aw, man," he says. "I forgot my debit card."

*

It's so late. I want to sleep. It's almost morning. I buy the Coke, and I buy him the cigarettes, and I take him to his apartment, but it's not what I want. I want a brand. I want to make cities. I want to know the secret language so I can take from other people. I have to go out there and take it. I'm a terrible liar. I need to learn to manage my money better. I'll eat what you buy me, obey the oracle, clean the vomit. I'll do it this way, myself. I have to do it this way. One day I'm born, the next day I'm dead. I have my seasons.

I used to be so pretty. I wish you could've seen me. You would've loved me.

On the Desire to Reject Narcissism*

*Notes Toward a Follow-Up Essay to "The Uber Diaries"

Opening #1:

When one writes an essay—when one writes anything (a story, a screenplay, a song, a tweet, a letter to a lover)—one reveals.

When one reads one's own essay (story, screenplay, song, tweet, letter), one must consider what one has revealed about oneself.

When one devolves, in referring to oneself, from the first person to the third, one must ask oneself: Why?

Because the distance that has been traveled from first to third is a distance that must be traveled with great effort. The sentence-making must travel away from the sharp elegance of narrative (subject-transitive verb-object) into the dark territory of the rhetorical (When one X's, then one might Y; If A, then B; If not B, then C or D, unless E . . .)

Or:

Opening #2:

But why does one need to be pretty? Why does one need to be seen? Why would one write an ending that equated the cry of the pink-hoodied cancer patient with the cry of the failed screenwriter driving the Uber Toyota?

Why the slow colonizing metastasis of the clotting "I" in the concluding section?

Consider the count:

Eighteen sentences, twenty-three independent or dependent clauses, sixteen nouns, fifteen active verbs (five of them wants, one a wish, one a need), two me's, twenty I's. More I's than sentences. More I's than nouns. More I's than active verbs.

Or:

Opening #3

Assignment:

1. Write a diptych of essays at least partially Holocaust adjacent.
2. Write an essay about the death of a friend, a story you consider to be personally sacred . . .
3. As though implying an equivalence, squeeze between them an essay about how hard it is to work a regular job in the Midwest instead of doing the exciting things you want to do to elevate your work to the attention of the world while living high on the hog in California.

Or:

Opening #5

TK Textbook definitions of narcissism:

Opening #8

It is good for a book to argue with itself?

It is good for a person to be of two minds, to hold two or three contradictory positions in tension at all times, to reject the stranglehold of ideology, to be humble enough to understand that the world needs different things at different times?

Opening #9

~~TK Susan Sontag writing *On Photography*, then writing *Regarding the Pain of Others* in partial refutation of *On Photography*.~~

Opening #9

> Witnessing requires the creation of star witnesses.
>
> —Susan Sontag, *Regarding the Pain of Others*

Opening #11

TK The story of Narcissus and Echo

The self-regarder requires an audience, who . . .

Opening #14

When one has primarily (and for a long time) been mostly keeping the company of fiction writers, poets, journalists, university professors, visual artists, and filmmakers, and then one suddenly finds oneself moving briskly through the city nightly in the company of bankers, lawyers, nurses, construction workers, food-service workers, sex workers, and bartenders, one begins to believe that the proportions of one's engagement with the world have become . . .

Opening #16

TK Something something about narcissism as the dominant trope (or at least the unexamined dark underbelly) of contemporary empowerment/therapeutic/"self-care" schemes.

Opening #23

NARCISSUS AND ECHO

a poem by Fred Chappell

Shall the water not remember *Ember*
my hand's slow gesture, tracing above *of*
its mirror my half-imaginary *airy*
portrait? My only belonging *longing,*
is my beauty, which I take *ache*
away and then return, as love *of*
of teasing playfully the one being *unbeing.*
whose gratitude I treasure *Is your*
moves me. I live apart *heart*
from myself, yet cannot *not*
live apart. In the water's tone, *stone?*
that shining silence, a flower *Hour,*
whispers my name with such slight *light:*
moment, it seems filament of air, *fare*
the world become cloudswell. *well.*

Opening #29

TK Had a brief thought about Tony Hoagland's *What Narcissism Means to Me* and lost it. (Look it up?)

Opening #31

Thinking about the general impulse to use ideological frameworks as distancing/denial mechanisms to avoid self-examination, in-cluding and especially in the traditional 21st c. "literary" sense . . .

Opening #36

Before indicting others, one must properly indict oneself.

To give twenty-three examples . . .

Opening #37

TK The cultural obsession with "being seen."

Opening #41

TK Maybe find the quote you read last week (*NY Review of Books*, maybe?, be sure to give attribution), something along the lines of:

> The protagonist of John Cheever's "The Swimmer" swims blissfully and uninhibitedly across all his neighbors' backyard pools, but when he reaches his own house, the front door has been locked against him.

TK Some discussion about why the front door has been locked against him, etc.

Opening #43

Are all writers of essays, stories, screenplays, songs, poems, tweets, letters narcissists?

Are some?

How many?

A few? Half? Most?

How can the reader distinguish one from the other?

Does it matter to the reader?

Should it?

How can one know if oneself is "one of those"?

Does it matter to oneself?

What now?

Opening (Ideas) #46

TK An opening about the years so many people I knew went to Nashville to make it big in the music business.

TK Nashville as a metaphor for New York publishing or Broadway or Hollywood or the Iowa Writers' Workshop.

TK The way they all joked they were "living the dream" while waiting tables or day-jobbing for the trucking logistics company or sleeping four to a van with their instruments and gear and the smelly road manager while the rich bandleader slept a block away in the luxury suite, etc.

TK The people who kept saying don't worry, it doesn't come right away, Nashville is a "ten year town."

TK The trust fund babies who had no problem swinging ten years with no income. The one of them who said, "You'd do better if you got some decent clothes."

TK The people who kept saying, "Are you crazy? Get a job that lets you eat regularly. Don't you want a home? Don't you want to provide for a family? What pathology is driving all this? Whatever it is, it's selfish. It's ugly."

TK Something more baldly and artlessly "What drives you?" something. Like: What is the unfilled space inside you that requires that stage, those lights, etc.?

TK Opening where the essay's subject buys a lottery ticket and thinks it's the same thing he or she is doing with his or her professional life every day: The next screenplay is the ticket. The next novel. The next song.

TK Psychedelic/cartoon opening, where a starving person pushes a demo tape through a hole in the side of a building on Music Row, and suddenly the sky opens up and rains money and designer food.

TK Fantasy opening, where the essay's subject imagines his or her father or mother finally understanding his or her pursuit and giving his or her approval, or every person with whom he or she went to high school calling to apologize for not noticing the great talent he or she had always embodied, and that the new record "just goddamn blew my mind."

TK Out of context, that line from Touré: "What's Inside You, Brother?"

TK Maybe quote the outro tag from that Hailey Whitters song, the greatest song ever written about the "chasing the dream" psychology of Nashville or New York publishing or Broadway or Hollywood or the Iowa Writers' Workshop:

This next song could turn it all around /
I'm twelve years into a ten year town.

Opening #47

TK Quote in full:

"Lose Yourself," by Eminem

i.e., "You only get one shot / Do not miss your chance to blow / This opportunity comes once in a lifetime."

Opening #48

TK, similar to the "Lose Yourself" opening, except it's about the one tune in every Broadway musical that tells you how this show is about the exact same thing as all the other Broadway musicals.

TK, second paragraph about how even *Hamilton* is about "I'm gonna be a big fabulous star now."

i.e., "In New York you can be a new man / just you wait."

and: "I am not throwing away my shot / I'm just like my country / I'm young, scrappy, and hungry / And I'm not throwing away my shot."

Opening #51

X called yesterday, upset that I had written about him.

What gives you the right?

Etc.

Opening #52

What is the responsibility of the narrative artist when his or her material traffics in the lives of others?

How are the choices that correspond with the answer to that question in conversation with the needs and exigencies of the work of art which lives (or will live) separately from the person who made it?

Does the work of art live separately from the person who made it?

To which of these is the artist's fidelity owed:

To the work or to the person?

Opening #52 (alternative break into white space)

To which of these is the fidelity of the human being who makes the art owed:

To the work, or to the other human being?

Opening #53

There is comfort in asking questions that can be easily answered.

There is comfort in the idea that questions can be easily answered.

There is discomfort in the idea that there is not always a single answer to any given question . . .

Opening #55

TK On the internet / social media / everyone now a star (do this in a quote?)

Opening #56

Are all heavy users of social media narcissists?

Are some?

How many?

A few? Half? Most?

How can the reader distinguish one from the other?

Does it matter to the reader?

Should it?

How can one know if oneself is "one of those"?

Does it matter to oneself?

What now?

Opening #60

TK Something ironic/countercultural on the idea of "boundaries" and how the kind of people who are always talking about them always seem to be kind of shitty to the other people in their lives?

Opening #61

TK Here find the quote from *NY Times* about the son who died because his mother believed the 12-step programs when they said instead of intervening, you should allow your children to reach "rock bottom" so they have a chance to kick their alcohol or drug habit.

Opening #63

One notices that those most likely to cause oneself injury are those who are most truly convinced of their own righteousness. No, this is not another essay about the Southern Baptists I knew as a child. Today I'd like to speak about my people to whom I fled as an adult seeking comfort and reason, the . . .

Opening #67

TK Some kind of clinical quote on narcissistic injury and suicide.

Opening #68

Late night, at a bar, late enough that people begin telling the truth even though it's almost always the wrong thing to do, to tell the truth in any semiprofessional situation, a writer my age, a person I very much admire, decries the common contemporary genre she or he describes as "someone hurt me a little bit, a long time ago."

Am I / have I been one of those?

Opening #69

~~Definition of "Professional": That state of being and interacting in which no one is unwise enough to tell the truth about anything that's going on, unless one wants to face severe and dramatic consequences.~~

Opening #69

Late night, at a bar, late enough that people begin telling the truth even though it's almost always the wrong thing to do, to tell the truth in any semiprofessional situation, a companion my age, a person who herself or himself survived a genocide, decries the writer who just went home for the evening after complaining loudly about X thing that now seems very small because of the knowledge everyone at the table shares about the personal history of the person who is now retracting the thing she or he has just said about the writer who departed, because it is less than generous, and it is wrong to be less than generous. Please forgive me.

Am I / have I been one of those?

Opening #71

It angers me when a person commits suicide and others take it as an opportunity to turn the tragedy into an object lesson.

The preacher who ends the eulogy with a call to repentance and salvation. The scold who shames the living who were unable to intervene and prevent the tragedy. The investigator who blames the family. The family that turns one upon another, in sorrow, in shock, in blame. The op-ed writer whose first paragraph describes the suicide and whose second paragraph describes a bill making its way through the legislature.

~~The only proper response to a suicide is to try to understand~~

~~One good way to respond to news of a suicide is to~~

~~There is nothing good to be said about a~~

Opening #72

THE ONLY ANIMAL

a poem by Franz Wright

The only animal that commits suicide
went for a walk in the park,
basked on a hard bench
in the first star,
traveled to the edge of space

in an armchair
while company quietly
talked, and abruptly
returned,
the room empty.

The only animal that cries,
that takes off its clothes
and reports to the mirror, the one
and only animal
that brushes its own teeth—

somewhere

the only animal that smokes a cigarette,
that lies down and flies backward in time,
that rises and walks to a book
and looks up a word
heard the telephone ringing
in the darkness downstairs and decided
to answer no more.

And I understand,
too well: how many times
have I made the decision to dwell
from now on
in the hour of my death
(the space I took up here
scarlessly closing like water)
and said I'm never coming back,

and yet

this morning
I stood once again
in this world, the garden
ark and vacant
tomb of what
I can't imagine,
between twin eternities,
some sort of wings,
more or less equidistantly
exiled from both,
hovering in the dreaming called
being awake, where
You gave me
in secret one thing
to perceive, the
tall blue starry
strangeness of being
here at all.
You gave us each in secret one thing to perceive.

Furless now, upright, My banished
and experimental
child

You said, though your own heart condemn you

I do not condemn you.

Opening #73

When Franz Wright was fourteen or fifteen years old, he wrote a poem and mailed it to his estranged father, James Wright, the greatest poet of his generation.

His father's reply:

I'll be damned. You're a poet. Welcome to hell.

Opening #74

I would like to open with the supposition that it's possible that the origin of suffering lies in the fierce need to be seen.

Opening #75

I would like to open with the supposition that it's possible that the origin of suffering lies in the fierce desire to have one's genius validated by others.

~~**Opening #75a**~~

~~When I think of these things I want to make myself disappear.~~

~~When I think of these things I want to make myself go away.~~

~~When I think of these things~~

~~**Opening #78**~~

~~I would like to open with the supposition that one measure of the nobility of a narrative artist's aspirations might be the intensity of his or her midcareer commitment to the choice to move out of the register of the purely personal preoccupation and into the realm of public discourse, for the purpose of making a good faith contribution rather than as a pragmatic path to further self-aggrandizement.~~

Opening #79

TK Find and quote statistics on narcissism by profession (beginning with poets)

Opening #83

TK Paragraph about how Susan Sontag wrote most of *Freud: The Mind of the Moralist*, the book upon which her eleven years older first husband Philip Rieff's scholarly reputation and academic career was founded, and how he never granted her proper credit.

Opening #84

> High-mindedness will not prevent the most terrible outbreaks of a violence that inverts the higher indifference. Narcissism will flower on the smallest differences. Despite its manifestos of grievances against the forms of higher authority, the movement toward secularity will be favored by the modern state. Therapies against authority serve the state's highest interest by releasing the nuclear energy of politics—namely, killing and being killed for the smallest reasons.
>
> —from *Freud: The Mind of the Moralist*,
> by Philip Rieff

Opening #85

TK One of those stories (pick any one) of Susan Sontag performing narcissistic behavior being performatively a narcissist from either (1) the Benjamin Moser biography, (2) the David Rieff memoir, (3) the Sigrid Nunez memoir, (4) . . .

Opening #86

TK Opening inquiry into the relationship between intelligence and narcissism.

~~**Opening #87**~~

~~TK Opening inquiry into the relationship between narcissism and sanctimony.~~

Opening #87

TK Opening inquiry into childhood wealth (and/or childhood lack) and narcissism.

Opening #88

TK Opening inquiry into the culturally mostly sanctioned wrongness of mistaking high-functioning autism for or conflating high-functioning autism with narcissism.

Opening #89

TK Opening inquiry into relationship between physical appearance and narcissism.

Opening #91

TK Exemplary story (find one?) on someone's rejection of their own acknowledged narcissism.

Opening #93

TK Inquiry into history of the evolving relationship between narcissism and Christianity.

Opening #96

TK Inquiry on Buddhist practice of renunciation as rejection of narcissism.

Opening #97

WHY I AM NOT A BUDDHIST

a poem by Molly Peacock

I love desire, the state of want and thought
of how to get; building a kingdom in a soul
requires desire. I love the things I've sought—
you in your beltless bathrobe, tongues of cash that loll
from my billfold—and love what I want: clothes,
houses, redemption. Can a new mauve suit
equal God? Oh no, desire is ranked. To lose
a loved pen is not like losing faith. Acute
desire for nut gateau is driven out by death,
but the cake on its plate has meaning,
even when love is endangered and nothing matters.
For my mother, health; for my sister, bereft,
wholeness. But why is desire suffering?
Because want leaves a world in tatters?
How else but in tatters should a world be?
A columned porch set high above a lake.
Here, take my money. A loved face in agony,
the spirit gone. Here, use my rags of love.

Opening #112

I'm trying to understand.

Is narcissism a fixed state? Is it a disease? A mental illness, like schizophrenia? If so, can it be medicated?

Or is it a description of behaviors? If so, can a person choose to change the behaviors?

Is it that the behavior is narcissistic, or is it that the person is a narcissist?

Is the behavior redeemable?

Is the person?

Opening #117

If a narcissist needs an audience . . .

If one is beginning to believe oneself to be a narcissist, and one wants to be other than a narcissist . . .

If one requires an audience in order to continue to be a narcissist . . .

What if one were to . . . simply . . . disappear from view of all plausible audiences . . .

If one were to disappear . . .

Opening #131

Excerpt from Tony Hoagland's poem "Argentina":

> How did I come to believe in a government called
> Tony Hoagland?
> with an economy based on flattery and self-protection?
> and a sewage system of selective forgetting?
> and an extensive history of broken promises?

Concluding Paragraph #5

TK The young man who just finished reading Solzhenitsyn's *The Gulag Archipelago* and *One Day in the Life of Ivan Denisovich*, telling everyone in his despair: What do I do now? It's making me crazy. I'll never be able to write a book like that.

TK The young woman who replied: Of course you can. It's easy. Just join the Red Army, denounce Stalin, spend eight years at forced labor in the Gulag, find yourself sentenced to exile-for-life in Kazakhstan, write the authoritative history of your repressive government's network of political prison labor camps, enjoy a brief reprieve from Khrushchev, fall out of favor again when Khrushchev dies, lose your citizenship and be declared a nonperson, win a Nobel Prize for Literature you are forbidden from traveling to Sweden to collect, move to America . . .

III.
(COWARDICE, CONFORMITY, COURAGE)

I closed my eyes once we were
ordered to sit down.

—Yiyun Li

The Lizard, the Stink, the Bear, the Game, the Road to Somewhere

1.

Here is a story where nothing happens:

2.

Yesterday a woman at my work walked up behind me and firmly put her hands on both of my shoulders.

In the fraction of a second between the moment in which she touched me and the moment in which I turned too quickly to face her, a tremendous invisible drama unfolded inside of me. My hands wanted to ball up into fists. My body wanted to barrel into hers. My limbic system wanted me to lead with a sharp elbow to the head, followed by a knee.

My task, as a civilized adult, was to soften myself, take a step backward instead of a step forward, convince myself that I was likeliest to turn and face a colleague rather than an assailant, and that if it was an assailant behind me, that the best thing I could do was take the blow, back away, retaliate not at all.

That's what I did, and for the last thirty years, that's what I've done.

At the end of the invisible drama, one second later, she said, *I must have really startled you.*

I guess so, I said.

Yeah, she said. F*or a second there, you had a crazy look on your face.*

She had seen the Lizard.

3.

The origin story of the Lizard begins in a puke-green locker room at the Christian school, where football equipment hung like meat in red bags from metal hooks.

For two prepubescent years, I walked into that room expecting every day to be punched in the face, punched in the arm, twisted by the arm, fingered in the ear, fingered in the armpit, slapped in the ear, slapped at the testicles, grabbed by the earlobe, grabbed by the nipples, pinched at the nipples, twisted at the nipples.

My hairless body was roughly half the size of the bodies of the punchers, fingerers, slappers, grabbers, pinchers, and twisters. It had been lifted against lockers, pressed against lockers, shoved into lockers. My head had been slammed into lockers, slammed against benches, submerged in toilet water.

(I don't want to talk about the other things that were shoved inside of me.)

After a while, since no one would make it stop, I stopped cowering and started swinging back. Fists, elbows, knees, the hard part of the head. If I could find something to grab, I'd grab it and swing it, too.

This made good sport for some of my assailants, but it made other people stop. I was small, but I had no fear in these moments. I was capable of hurting people, too. Sometimes, when I thought about it later, it seemed that I—whatever I was—had gone away altogether, and some other presence was running my body in its place. A dark, angry, sinister presence.

Ordinary people would back away from the Lizard.

4.

If you are reading this essay, you probably hold at least a bachelor's degree. It's not unlikely that you have a master's degree or a PhD.

That doesn't mean you're my ideal reader. It just means that you're probably the reader that I have, because people like you—(and, I suppose, people like me)—are the people likeliest to read a book of essays.

But the culture of books of essays and the people likeliest to read them sits uncomfortably against the kind of culture that spawns something like the Lizard.

So I am afraid, asking you to look at this unpleasant thing, that I am losing you.

Maybe that's not true.

Maybe you're a person—like me—who went to college and slowly realized that your most immediately important task was not learning about the humanities and the arts and the sciences and the social sciences.

Your most immediately important task was learning the culture of the place, which is to say learning the culture of a different, socially higher class of Americans that isn't fully aware of its cultural difference from, say, people like you were at age eighteen. Because it isn't aware, it expects you to know the rules of engagement, which are not the only rules of engagement in America. And yet, if you don't learn to engage by these rules, it will not matter what you've learned about the humanities and the arts and the sciences and the social sciences, because you will not be allowed to gain access to the monetization of what you've learned. To the class, to the culture.

Here is a partial list of things I did not know when I entered college:

5.

1. What to say.
2. What not to say.
3. How to say it.
4. How to say it to whom.
5. How not to say it to whom.
6. When to speak.
7. When not to speak.
8. What to do with your hands and body in various social situations.
9. How to properly sit in a chair.
10. How to properly laugh in a group of people.
11. What people mean when they say things that aren't exactly what they mean.
12. What a joke is.
13. What a joke isn't.
14. What a threat is when it is not a physical threat.
15. How to dress in various social situations.
16. How to style hair in various social situations.
17. How to know who is in charge.
18. How to know when it is or isn't time to be in charge.

19. How to be in charge.
20. How to be when not in charge.
21. The nature of the interpersonal politics of the new people.
22. The nature of the electoral politics of the new people.
23. How to speak or not speak about the old people while around the new people.
24. How to get the list of opinions important to getting along with the new people, which has great overlap with the list of opinions to avoid when trying to get along with the old people.
25. How to not react to things in a visibly discernable manner.
26. How to not walk around with your head, as they say, on a swivel.
27. How to strategically hide your hand.
28. How to behave at a party.
29. How to leave a party early, even if you are having a good time.
30. How to identify who is the target the group plans to banish, when nobody is hitting that person.
31. How to know if you are or might be becoming the target.

6.

If you master these rules, you might master them incompletely.

Or you might master them completely enough to climb a rung of the class ladder, but then you will encounter a further refinement of these rules, and you must begin to learn them again.

As you climb the ladder, you will begin to notice that someone keeps raising and lowering the ceiling, depending upon who is climbing.

7.

You might be, for example, at a party at the prestigious graduate school to which you've somehow gained admission a full ten years after the first time you were rejected.

This party might even be in your honor.

(Let's say your book of short stories has been accepted for publication.)

You might have recently returned from the Michigan Reformatory, where you have been interviewing a man some call the Halloween Killer of Kalamazoo. You have not spent a lot of time with this man, but you've spent time enough to know that he has kicked the drugs that made him crazy. Although he is serving a life sentence, he is trying his best to redeem his life. His children are growing into adults in a place far away from him. One of them will not speak with him. He is trying to find ways to get them some money to pay for college.

He speaks to you honestly about the night he became a murderer. His job was to travel and sell, but the shocks in his car were blown. After a certain number of miles, his back began to hurt. Painkillers became heroin—it took some months for one to become the other—and the downer of heroin required a strong upper. Eventually, on Halloween night, he drives to Kalamazoo, trades his car for crack, and proceeds to get higher than he ever could have imagined possible. Blitzed, ripped, flying. In the fog that follows, he buys a pistol, breaks down the door of a rooming house, tries to bum some booze and cigarettes. It happens so fast—a noise, a vibration, a feeling—he panics and pulls the trigger. It isn't until later he understands what it means that a stranger is dead. That he's killed a man. He doesn't even leave. When the police arrive, they find him sitting on the floor, drinking one of the stolen beers.

On the drive to and from the Michigan Reformatory, you ask yourself: Of all the stories to try to tell, why this murderer's story?

You're thinking about Anton Chekhov, who took the train to the Siberian prison colony for Russian exiles at Sakhalin Island in 1890, to witness *the extreme limits of man's degradation* and bring the news back to Russia. His report was full of beatings, floggings, slave labor, starvation, women forced into a brutal regime of prostitution likened to a cattle market. Widespread syphilis. Gangrenous limbs. Widespread blindness from untreated conjunctivitis. Rumors of cannibalism. Dead babies. Dozens forced to sleep in a single filthy cell. A little girl sleeping with her wife-murdering father for warmth in a heap of prisoners.

The book Chekhov wrote led to the partial abolishment of the exile system by order of Tsar Nicholas II in 1899—the public outcry forced the tsar's hand—although it would later roar back a hundredfold in the new Soviet form Solzhenitsyn called *The Gulag Archipelago*. The public outcry was too much.

Your own prison conversation yields lower-wattage outrages. Your prisoner says living at the Michigan Reformatory is like being sentenced for life to wait in the lobby of the Department of Motor Vehicles. Same plastic bucket chairs, same uniformed bureaucrat in a chair with the power to make you wait until your name is called, except—if you're serving a life sentence—it's not an afternoon you're slow-burning. It's the rest of your life.

Quickly, though, he moves past complaint. What he really seems to want from you is to talk about books. Novels, especially. He's well-versed in literary fiction—he studied it at Western Michigan University—but what he really loves is science fiction. Big ideas, big metaphors, big world-building. He's writing two books—a book of literary short stories about prison, which he'll later sell to a New

York publisher, and a science fiction novel, which no one wants to touch. He's acquainted with the romantic tradition of the prisoner-writer—Jean Genet, Henri Charrière, Malcolm Braly—and he's pragmatic enough to know that the prison stories, which he sees as a kind of pandering, are his best chance to funnel some cash to his kids.

When you leave, he begs you to visit again, call him on the phone, send him some books.

A friend—a person you know who knows a thing or two about prison—says your prisoner is snowing you. Reeling you in. Soon he'll be asking you to put money on his commissary account. Soon he'll be sending a member of the Aryan Brotherhood, the white supremacist gang, to your door. *Let the extortion begin,* your friend says.

But you're growing tired of writing about the puke-green locker room, the red equipment bags, etc. The childhood grievances. Inside you there's a vague but growing idea—a newly unfashionable idea—that literature should try to take on the trouble of the world. Not just the local trouble of people who look and think like you. That a writer should try to spend time with other kinds of people living other kinds of lives. Suspend judgment long enough to listen. Really try to stretch out into understanding. Earn it hard. Do it again and again. See if there are things to be uncovered by reading across the different ways of being in the world. The different circumstances, different limitations, different joys, different worldviews.

It's not that you know how to do it. You don't. But you've spent a lot of time and money trying. Up and down the Danube River, in an agricultural village in rural Haiti, in a Port-au-Prince terrorized by kidnappers, in eastern Kentucky hollows, in latter-day sugar plantations in Florida, in courthouses and archives and library microfilm rooms, in a low-rent Ohio veterinary office, scrubbing in for the ovariohysterectomy of a cat enslaved for nine years in a tiny cage at a kitten mill.

You might be standing at the refrigerator at this party, drinking a beer. The other people in the kitchen might be telling stories about parties like these—at Harvard, Yale, Stanford, Oxford, Cambridge, the Sorbonne—places you've never visited that loom large in your imagination. A curious feeling might creep in. You might feel like your work has earned you the opportunity to belong.

A classmate might appear, wearing a three-hundred-dollar dress, a few hours off the plane from a weekend in Paris.

When she speaks, the other people in the room stop talking.

Someone hands her a bottle, and she pops the top. Her power cannot be denied. She knows celebrities, famous writers, the founders of Silicon Valley start-ups. Young ones, old ones. Sometimes they come to town to see her. Sometimes they attend parties and you see them there. All the people on three continents with the keys to the dreams of the people in this room seem to know and listen to her. She seems to have inexhaustible amounts of money. She never wears an inexpensive outfit, and she never seems to wear the same outfit twice. While other classmates share portions of subdivided houses, she commands the master bedroom of one of the biggest houses in the center of town. Big dining area. Big backyard. Big parties. Big music. Her attention is intoxicating. Her scorn is more than withering.

Now it is directed at you.

I've heard you've been writing about a murderer, she says. *Have you reached out to the family of the man he murdered?*

She takes a long performative swig of the beer.

You need to read some more elegant books, she says. *Learn about metaphor. Chekhov, you know? You think you're reading about an affair on an island between two unhappy people. Mismatched people. A misogynist banker and a young woman walking her dog. You think it's some kind of sad love story. But what you're really getting—in microcosm—is the spiritual history of all of Russia.*

Then she is gone. The other people in the kitchen back away from you.

You walk home alone.

8.

On the walk home, that evening in bed, in the years ahead, you think about what you could have said:

Don't you know that Chekhov was so passionate about visiting the prisoners at Sakhalin Island that he got on the train from Moscow even though he knew he was sick with the tuberculosis that killed him? An eleven-week journey over the most remote terrain in the Northern Hemisphere. Then three months in the camp, in the cold, in an incubator for the worst contagions in the world. And he was a medical doctor!

9.

You didn't say it because you were right not to say it.

This is progress.

It cost her nothing to embarrass you, but what would it have cost you to embarrass her?

10.

But the encounter costs you something anyway, or you imagine it does.

The people who backed away—your Ivied peers in the kitchen—

stay backed away.

You don't blame them. Not entirely. It is a tenuous thing to be in the orbit of this powerful classmate who is capable of casting people away so easily. Their strategy is validated by time. You watch the whole cohort step into powerful positions in book publishing, magazines, media. They publish and nurture the careers of their talented friends, some of whose names and faces you are now seeing in magazine profiles, as guests on late-night TV shows, in the credits of prestige cable dramas and movies.

No one is blackballing you. It's more like you're starting to realize you smell wrong. Like they know about the weekends spent on job sites while your father repaired air conditioners, the Sunday nights listening from church pews to the traveling preachers of the Apocalypse, the days of childhood illness spent watching war movies and Westerns with your grandfather in your grandmother's trailer while your mother assisted the kindergarten teacher and drove the school bus.

You've got the stink.

11.

You resolve to partially embrace the stink.

Resolve to let it into your work. Make it part of your project.

Otherwise, in all the other parts of your life, you hide the stink as best you can. Time passes. You say less and less.

12.

You look for models.

When you find them, you compare yourself to them and feel there is some distance yet to be traveled.

Edwidge Danticat, Zadie Smith, Richard Price, Yiyun Li,

Nam Le, Isaac Babel, Percival Everett, William Faulkner, Dany Laferrière, Haruki Murakami.

People writing about people who are like the people they have known, or who are like the people they might have otherwise been, even if those people are deemed beneath some momentarily powerful audience's attention. People writing broadly about the world out of a particular context, but who are unafraid to inhabit the point of view of the ostensible "monster," or to extend their imaginative empathy in the direction of whomever might be deemed "Other." People trying to lean hard into complication and contradiction. People trying to synthesize. People willing to risk being wrong in the service of searching for what is true. People trying to understand.

You're reading a book about Joseph Conrad, by a Harvard history professor named Maya Jasanoff. Unlike most academic historians, she writes sentences that sing. There's real power in her point of view. She describes herself as a half-Asian, half-Jewish woman writing complicatedly about a dead white man capable of underselling women, exoticizing Asians, and offering up the occasional anti-Semitic trope or turn of phrase.

On a journey around the world, following in Conrad's footsteps through Poland and Congo, doing the work of reading him in the context of his historical moment, her regard for Conrad grows. As a baby, he is christened by a Ukrainian friar in 1857, in a city that used to belong to the Polish-Lithuanian commonwealth, but now belongs to the Russian Empire. Russia has taken most of Lithuania, Belarus, and Ukraine, too. What remains of the rest of the Polish state has been seized by Austria and Prussia. Conrad's father's christening song begins: *To my son, born in the 85th year of Muscovite oppression.*

The political instability continues for Conrad's entire childhood. His family is at the center of the nationalist resistance, so the Russians make them no strangers to arrest and imprisonment. His mother dies of tuberculosis. His exiled father teaches him to read in five languages. As a teenager, he joins the French merchant marine. Four years later, he joins the English merchant marine. In fifteen years, sailing every ocean in the world, he works his way up from lowly steward to captain.

Slowly, he's becoming British. His voyages take him to places invisible to the people in the capitals of the European empires that loot and abuse them. Congo, Borneo, Bangkok, the Gulf of Mexico, the Caribbean, Singapore, Malaysia, India, Australia, South America.

Slowly, he's becoming something not just British and Polish. The world is leaking into him. Languages, places, ways of seeing. Methods of wealth extraction. Methods of work. The ivory trade. The rubber trade. Cargo. Spycraft. The hazards of boats. The textures of objects. The differences in the ways places taste and smell. The monstrosity of unchecked human nature.

And so it's all in the novels, which together form a kind of shadow history of the late nineteenth- and early twentieth-century colonial world, in detail no historian has equaled, by a man born into a nationality that did not officially exist.

As Jasanoff writes:

The world is made of "nowheres" and "somewheres"—but which counts as which depends on what "where" you look from. The story of [Conrad's] life, and the world in which he lived, was a story of nowheres colliding with somewheres.

13.

Your mother mails a direct-to-video Disney movie to your son.

Pooh's Heffalump Movie.

The first time he watches, you don't. Nothing could be more benign—or more boring—than the pleasant adventures of Piglet, Tigger, Eeyore, Rabbit, Roo, and Winnie the Pooh.

But then it's over and he's red-eyed. You ask what's wrong. *The animals,* he says. *What they did is terrible.*

So you start it again. Whatever you expected, it's not what you're seeing.

What you're seeing is an animated Winnie the Pooh musical about genocide, with a soundtrack of original pop songs by Carly Simon. It begins like this:

14.

There is a strange noise in the Hundred Acre Wood.

There are footprints. They are large. *What creature could be attached to a foot that big?* Pooh asks.

There's only one thing it could be, Rabbit says. *A Heffalump.*

15.

The music swells dramatically.

The citizens of the Hundred Acre Wood, none of whom have ever seen a Heffalump, sing a song of fearful speculation.

They work themselves up into such a frenzy that it begins to seem necessary to organize an expedition to find and capture the Heffalump before it does any real damage to the peace of the Hundred Acre Wood.

Rabbit, the self-appointed vigilante ringleader, deputizes Tigger, Pooh, Piglet, and Eeyore, arms them with lassos, swears them in. Their young friend Roo wants to join the mission, but Rabbit won't allow it, because the Heffalump hunt is too dangerous for a baby kangaroo.

While they're hunting, Roo strikes out on his own. He finds and befriends a baby Heffalump named Lumpy and brings him home to the Hundred Acre Wood. They play rough and tear up Pooh's house and Rabbit's garden.

When Rabbit's expeditionary force returns home empty-handed, they find the wreckage in house and garden. The Heffalump invasion is on, they decide.

They set traps. They are militant in tone and intention.

One fears for the Heffalump.

And one is right to fear.

In the end, baby Lumpy, after being trapped in a cage, lassoed, and detained by the now-deranged and plausibly homicidal citizen-mob of the Hundred Acre Wood, is only saved after Roo falls into a pile of logs covering a bottomless pit as a kind of makeshift bridge.

To save the baby kangaroo, the baby Heffalump calls for his mother, who is able, because of her strong elephant-like trunk, to lift away the heavy top logs that have kept the others from reaching and saving him before he falls to his death in the abyss.

It's a happy ending only in the sense that order is restored to the Hundred Acre Wood before the genocide can begin. Because the viewer—even a child like my son—has the clear and disconcerting sense that Winnie the Pooh and his friends had every intention of eradicating every last Heffalump from the face of the earth.

16.

Once you start thinking about genocide as a theme in children's stories, books, and movies, you begin to see it everywhere.

Like it's elemental.

Like it sits naturally in the nature of humans as a dramatic sequence—the devaluing of the other, the scapegoating of some convenient other, eventually the possibility of genocide—alongside the basic questions of childhood: love, family, friendship, community, teamwork, growing up, problem-solving, loss, loneliness, fairness, compassion, kindness, truth-telling . . .

In Dr. Seuss's *Horton Hears a Who!*, the near eradication of a tiny planet on a speck of dust, if not for the intervention of an elephant named Horton, whose motto is "A person's a person, no matter how small."

In C. S. Lewis's *The Lion, the Witch and the Wardrobe*, the near eradication of all the talking animal races of Narnia, if not for the intervention of four British children who have entered the country through a magical wardrobe at the behest of a god-lion.

In the Death Eaters of *Harry Potter*, in the Roma genocide as seen through the eyes of the animals in *The Midnight Zoo*, in the Holocaust allegory of *The Hunger Games* . . .

17.

Pooh's Heffalump Movie, of course, is mistitled, for reasons you don't know but can imagine. Marketing imperatives, fear of scrutiny, laziness. The rightful title would be *Brownshirts in the Hundred Acre Wood.*

You imagine the work of cultural criticism—the missed opportunity to *show us something about ourselves*—as penned by Rebecca Solnit or Hilton Als or Tom Wolfe or Zadie Smith.

You imagine the subjects adjacent: the too-recent genocides in Darfur, Rwanda, Bosnia, Cambodia, and Armenia, apartheid in South Africa and Gaza and the eighty years of Jim Crow in the American South, Mao's Cultural Revolution, Stalin's destruction of the seed grain to starve the Ukrainians, the mobilization of Hitler's Brownshirts as a precursor to the Holocaust.

You sketch out a few objects for analysis:

1. The story made for children, which is not afraid to look at the monstrosity of human tendency, so long as it is allegorized.
2. The children who recognize the monstrosity at the center of the allegorized story.
3. Their outrage, directed rightly at the monstrosity, but not at the story.

You imagine a cautionary ending like the one Harry Crews wrote about University of Texas tower shooter Charles Whitman, the kind that implicates reader and writer alike:

But take a look around. Think about the last time you found a convenient person upon whom to purge the collective blame. At home, at school, in the neighborhood, the discourse, the workplace. Listen to your own memories. Listen to history.

There are Brownshirts in every Hundred Acre Wood.

18.

In your first university teaching job, your supervisor was a Marianne Moore, Elizabeth Bishop, and Wallace Stevens scholar, a fiercely intelligent woman in her sixties whose syllabus warning you adopt at the top of your own:

> **Literature concerns itself with the extremes of human behavior. Expect to read frankly about all varieties of human trouble, including but not limited to: God, war, sex, family, religion, genocide, geographic displacement, the body, physical and emotional violence, politics, coercion, and death.**

You ask her about the syllabus warning.

I consider it an invitation to adult life, she says.

19.

But within the last ten years, something has changed.

Any time a student has felt exceptional discomfort with a reading, you've always allowed them to opt out, in deference to the reality of unresolved trauma. Sure as shit you've got some of your own.

You notice other teachers nationwide getting in big trouble because they said something that made a student uncomfortable. You notice that when it comes time to defend the pedagogical position that informed the statement that brought the trouble—a recounting of someone else's historical position, a postulation about a literary character's point of view or state of mind, a temporarily pursued devil's advocacy in an attempt to invite students to imagine an interior life or a way of being in the world contrary to one's own—the context seems not to matter. Not the context, not the pedagogical imperative, not the intention. The bringing of discomfort is the actionable transgression.

20.

But what is the role of literature if not to bring the discomfort into the light? You're imagining the discomfort white Southern readers must have felt when reading James Baldwin's expert ventriloquizing of the racist Mississippi sheriff's childhood memories of watching a lynching on his father's shoulders in his story "Going to Meet the Man." You're imagining the discomfort progressive postwar Japanese readers must have felt when the right-wing virtuoso Yukio Mishima, in his story "Patriotism," laid bare the ugliness of the then-still-romanticized point of view of the emperor death cult that would later culminate in Mishima's own public ritual suicide.

21.

Nothing has happened to you.

No one has told you that there will be any consequences for teaching the way you've always taught. No one has told you that there will be any consequences for writing the way you aspire to write, allowing all the contradictions, peccadillos, and prejudices of your characters to exist alongside their capacities for generosity, decency, and nobility, the same way they do in the lived experiences of every person and every society in human history.

And yet:

You start talking less in class. Giving less. *Teaching* less.

And yet:

You notice that the fear that has caused you caution in the classroom is beginning to leak into the act of writing. That there is a new impediment to your desire to join the conversation of literature, and that the primary driver of impediment is inside your own self.

Your colleagues near and far don't seem particularly concerned. In fact, they seem broadly to embrace the new caution. When the COVID-19 epidemic begins, you are chastised for sharing with colleagues Katherine Anne Porter's "Pale Horse, Pale Rider," a novella narrated from the point of view of a young woman inhabiting a fever dream inside the analogous 1918 global pandemic then known as the Spanish flu, because the sharing of the novella exacerbates the general feeling of anxiety. You notice that instructively "problematic" texts are disappearing broadly from syllabi, replaced with newer work less likely to bring offense or contain perceived systemic wrongness. You notice that some of your students are emboldened by the project of identifying the wrongnesses, but that an increasing number of them seem afraid to take a position on many questions, to attempt any opinion at all, and that their fear mostly seems to be a fear of the other people in the room. You notice a change in the way controversial and offensive ideas are combated. In the past, the default mode was a robust engagement with the offensive idea, on the theory that the better idea would win the day on its merits.

You know from your own life's experience how often the better idea has won the day, culturally if not politically. You are proud to have participated in the campaign to elect the first African American president, not least because he was the smartest, most capable, and most trustworthy candidate of your lifetime, and later, in the failed campaign to elect the first American president who is a woman, although you believe that very soon there will be an American president who is a woman. You are proud to have marched on behalf of the right of gay people to marry, a victory that was accomplished in 2015. You wish someone—anyone—would summon the will to do something about generational poverty. You are worried about the rise of fascist-seeming demagoguery on the American right, a force that is asserting itself with great power. But you're cheered by what seems to be a cultural consensus among people your age and younger that seems inevitably to render a bleak future for this brand of demagoguery, despite the inevitable two-steps-forward, one-step-back progress of democracy.

But you notice that the wellsprings of cultural power—the universities, the public-facing parts of corporations, the journalists, the literary writers—are rapidly abandoning the notion that good ideas, through robust engagement, can defeat destructive ideas. The new notion that is replacing the old one requires that speech deemed to be wrong be deprived of oxygen, if possible, before it reaches the ears it might offend.

There is a tremendous inconsistency in the way these matters are policed. The demagogues have their own platforms. The nastier their messaging, it seems, the more their constituencies reward them. But on the other side of the ideological divide—among the people to whom you fled as a young person—small transgressions of speech, idea, or behavior that intersect with the wrong mob at the right time are ending careers, engendering broad public ridicule, exiling the identified representative transgressor—the one imperfect person among hundreds of thousands—to a life without friends. Or, given the polarization of the contemporary historical moment, exiling many a transgressor to a life without a people. It sounds hyperbolic, except you're watching it happen several times a week, sometimes to people you know.

Who would want to become one of those people?

22.

You detect around these questions a manipulatable quality.

A paranoia.

You notice that people whose ideas are anathema to your own are using what you hope is a temporary cultural overreach to bolster their own power.

Also:

You don't want to be on the wrong side of history. You're capable of being wrong. You find yourself being wrong all the time. You know you're a product of your time, no doubt still a carrier of unexamined notions that embarrassing experience will eventually unravel, if you are lucky.

You try to think it through.

23.

The list you make is tentative, incomplete.

Reading your own thoughts, you're disgusted by how many of them are self-serving, self-protective, self-centered, cowardly, apparently wrong.

The trash can is two feet away. You wad up the paper upon which you've written the list into a ball. Shoot a basket. Miss. Shoot again. Miss again.

A character flaw manifests: Everything to you is a metaphor.

In the real world, where objects are objects, the paper ball has come partially unrolled. You pick up the paper and read the list again.

There's a preoccupation you can't shake in Item #5.

24.

Here's the first half of the preoccupation:

As a child you were raised in a world where cultural inheritances you didn't even understand to be cultural inheritances—because they were, quite simply, the whole of the world you knew—intersected with great force:

1. The Southern Baptists, your religious denomination of origin, who split away from the northern Baptists because they could not abide the northern Baptists' opposition to American slavery, and who selectively punished violations of the community orthodoxies of speech or action by removing the violator from participation in the closed community, effectively cutting him or her off from everyone in his or her life.
2. The Apocalyptic prophecy people, who weaved in and out of all the ostensibly Christian communities you inhabited, insisting that the end of the world was drawing near, that sinners would be condemned to the coming terror of the

worldwide reign of the Antichrist, that to think a wrong thought was to sin as badly as to commit the corresponding wrong deed, and that, therefore, a person must constantly police and purge one's own thoughts to avoid Seven Years of terror on earth followed by an eternity of flesh-rending torment in the literal Lake of Fire.

3. The fundamentalists at the immersive Christian school you attended from age three until graduation at age seventeen, who required uniformity of clothing, manners, speech, and thought, and who selectively punished certain violations of the community orthodoxies of speech or action with expulsion from the closed community, effectively cutting off the violator from almost every peer he or she had ever known.

25.

Here's the second half of the preoccupation:

When you fled the Southern Baptists, the Apocalypse people, the fundamentalists, you meant to flee to the people who opened up the floor for conversation.

(This—the floor opened for conversation—is, in fact, the way that you came to the tentative understanding that one half of what you fled was irrational and the other half was in the service of preserving the status quo that served the powerful.)

When you fled the Southern Baptists, the Apocalypse people, the fundamentalists, you meant to flee the idea that to think or say it wrong was to be eternally cast out.

When you fled, it was to the world of the progress of ideas, which always transgress before they become accepted or acceptable. To the world of the university, where people who disagreed could gather in a public place and work it out, or at least offer their strident positions and air them to the scrutiny of the people in the room who are spending the first four years of their adulthood trying to work it out.

Most of all, to literature, which so rewired your brain that for a while you had unconsciously adopted it as a new kind of religion, with an enormous and contradictory library of scriptures that declared themselves fallible even before they began their project of demonstrating the irreconcilability of all things, sometimes in the pursuit of some measure of reconciliation, sometimes not.

26.

You're circling something.

Not an idea half-formed, but a lot of ideas half-formed.

A slow-gathering storm system of impressions, personal responses, incomplete understandings of what is happening in the world around you, personal pathologies, generalizations from your own uncommon experiences, inheritances constructive and destructive, relative and irrelative, consequential and benign.

All these abstractions, and plenty more, although everything seems increasingly to attach to questions about one word.

27.

Conformity: The prerequisite, in many cases, for belonging to a people.

Conformity: The barrier to overcoming prejudices, misunderstandings, and counterproductive habits of mind and action received from others.

Conformity: A necessity for maintaining social order, a situation of nonviolence, a coherent way for people to be together in the world.

Conformity: A weapon to be wielded.

Conformity: A shelter.

Conformity: A method of hiding from perceived danger.

Conformity: A desirable state which, once attained, might enable some motion up ladders of class, money, and position.

Conformity: A desirable state which, once attained, might replace the general uncertainty surrounding life's ever-changing and often irreconcilable contradictions with a kind of community-sanctioned certainty that can come to pass for hope.

Conformity: An undesirable reality to be pacified or contended against while trying to improve one's place in a sometimes-invisibly class-dominated society or culture.

Conformity: A force that destroys ideas, independence, literature.

Conformity: A stabilizing expectation that keeps a lot of bad things from happening in any given social system. A method of putting a lid on bad actors.

Conformity: A method of drawing a line of demarcation between the sweet and the stink.

Conformity: A strategy for avoiding discomfort.

Conformity: A tool that enables a social order to bend to the will of someone or something, in the service of either a present or future status quo.

28.

A few weeks ago I read a ten-year-old story by Nathan Englander.

"What We Talk About When We Talk About Anne Frank."

In the story, which is a kind of riff on Raymond Carver's "What We Talk About When We Talk About Love," two Jewish couples in

South Florida play the *Anne Frank game* in the wake of the terrorist attacks of 9/11:

> "It's the Righteous Gentile game," Shoshana says.
>
> "It's Who Will Hide Me?" I say.
>
> "In the event of a second Holocaust," Deb says, giving in. "It's a serious exploration, a thought experiment that we engage in."
>
> "That you play," Shoshana says.
>
> "That, in the event of an American Holocaust, we sometimes talk about which of our Christian friends would hide us."

When I was an undergraduate, one of my professors asked the same kind of question in a religion class. If you had been a citizen of Germany, Poland, Austria, when the Nazis came to power, would you have risked your life to speak up on behalf of the Jews? The Roma? Homosexuals? The infirm? Would you have risked the lives of your children to hide them? Would you have risked your job, your income, your house?

As I recall, every hand in the class went up, mine included.

Of course we would. Anyone would.

29.

These are dangerous questions my professor asked.

These questions put me and my classmates in a situation of discomfort so extreme that I am sweating right now, typing and remembering. I believe that these are vitally important questions. These questions have returned to me unbidden many times in bed, at night, in the dark. To interrogate them is to interrogate human nature as recorded in not-very-old history. Why is it that every person in that class could be absolutely, unhesitatingly certain that they would risk their lives to intervene in the darkest chapter of European history's darkest moment, and yet almost no one in Germany did?

I never ask my students questions like these anymore.

30.

Q: Why?

A: Because I lack the courage.

Q: What are you afraid of?

A: I don't want to lose my job, my income, my house . . .

31.

A realization creeps in:

What you're documenting is your own shame.

You lack an airtight argument, anything like a conclusion, even a hypothesis. The only surety is a feeling that something is wrong, that something has been very wrong for a long time, that somehow, in an effort to reach for a certain kind of life, you have disappeared into whatever it is that's wrong.

(*How long,* you hyperbolically postulate, *until you hunt the Heffalump?*)

All these small capitulations along the way in an effort to climb to somewhere from nowhere. Strategic silences. Pandering agreements. Laughing at the joke that's not funny. Not laughing at the joke that is funny. Speaking up for one kind of person but not for another. Using the word that placates power instead of the true word that divides the room.

32.

Q: How will you know who has the power?

A: Ask who has the power to set the rules of engagement.

33.

This morning—over 164 years after the birth of Joseph Conrad—Russian troops overran the borders of Ukraine. In Xinjiang, as many as two million Uyghurs are imprisoned in forced labor "reeducation" camps.

So far I've had nothing to say.

34.

I want to learn to be less careful with my words.

Hiding in Plain Sight

If you lived in Washington, DC, in the early 1960s, you might not have noticed the middle-aged Polish immigrant who was fixing up and flipping nineteenth-century row houses in the neighborhoods south of the Capitol. You wouldn't know that his burgeoning career in the Polish diplomatic corps had been derailed by a late-night knock at the door in August 1939, conscription orders a few days before the German Luftwaffe bombed, strafed, and destroyed the staging grounds at Oświęcim from the sky.

Even if you knew enough about history to know that this battle was the beginning of the end for the Polish army, you wouldn't know that the man now swinging the hammer, demolishing the plastered walls, laying linoleum over the old wood flooring, was among the first to know that this was the day Polish Oświęcim would become German Auschwitz, as he fled with his men through a city whose ethnic Germans, civilians of the newly constituted Nazi fifth column, stood at their apartment windows with rifles and rained sniper fire upon the Polish soldiers, some of whom were their neighbors.

If you stood in line behind this man at the hardware store, wondering why he bought his electrical wiring and his light fixtures at an unadvertised discount, you wouldn't know that he'd narrowly escaped a Soviet prisoner of war camp by pretending to be an enlisted man so the Soviets would trade him to the Germans, that he'd narrowly escaped the Germans by jumping out the window of a moving train, that he'd traveled northward by foot without a coat through a cold November, all the way back to a Warsaw so reduced to rubble that it hardly seemed anymore to be Warsaw at all.

As he signed his name—Jan Karski—in the store credit ledger, and walked to the lumber yard to retrieve his two-by-fours, you wouldn't have known (how could you have known?) that he wasn't born Jan Karski, that of all the names given to him by the Polish Underground—Kanicki, Kucharski, Kwasniewski, Witold, Znamirowski—Jan Karski was simply the one that stuck. You wouldn't know that in 1943, after he had traveled to pre-Vichy Paris to report on German atrocities to the Polish government-in-exile, after a second such journey ended in arrest and torture by the Gestapo in Slovakia, after he was smuggled by Jewish leaders into the Warsaw Ghetto and the death camp transit station at Izbica Lubelska to serve as an eyewitness. Or that he traveled first to London (disguised as a dental patient), then to the United States (as a Polish envoy), to try to warn the leaders of the Western world about the systematic killing of all the Jews in Poland.

You wouldn't know, because he wouldn't have told you.

Because he had disappeared into a life. Four days a week, a professor in the School of Foreign Service at Georgetown University. Three days a week, a self-taught carpenter, electrician, plumber, real estate trader. All those nights, to save money, sleeping in an illegally subdivided apartment in whichever of the row houses he was renovating.

He was hiding in plain sight.

He had his reasons.

*

It is not easy to hide in plain sight.

It takes work. Forethought. It can be learned.

When the British got into the guerilla warfare business in 1940, the watchwords were espionage, sabotage, and reconnaissance. Spies-in-training memorized the Special Operations Executive manual, whose primary obsession was the craft of hiding in plain sight:

> Your cover is the life which you outwardly lead in order to conceal the real purpose of your presence and the explanation which you give of your past and present. . . .
>
> The agent should merge into the background and act in the same way as those around him. This does not mean perpetual silence—which might be even more conspicuous—but natural behavior. Build up good reputation—be pleasant to people and avoid annoying them. Conform to local conditions.

All the professional armies of the Second World War honored the long traditions of military camouflage. They covered their machines and bodies to match the landscape. Green in forest and jungle, khaki in the desert, white in the snow.

The British and the Americans made use of the work of

Cambridge zoologist Hugh B. Cott, whose *Adaptive Coloration in Animals* described the visual manipulations by which animals made themselves safely inconspicuous:

> The coloration that resembles and the coloration that disrupts.
>
> The pattern that unsettles and the pattern that mimics and deceives.
>
> The shading that obliterates and the shadow that conceals.

*

Upon his return to Warsaw in November 1939, after his escapes from the Germans and the Soviets, Karski was deputized by his brother Marian Kozielewski, the commander of the Polish state police and the chief of security for the city of Warsaw. The policeman's uniform provided Karski great freedom to travel unmolested throughout occupied Poland, to observe and report and run errands for the nascent Polish Underground and for Marian's conspiracy of policemen, code name POL Insurance Co.

In Łódź, city of his birth, Poles who spoke aloud any language other than German were denied food. As German settlers moved in, Poles were given two hours to give up their homes. The Gestapo ordered Karski's uncle to leave a vase of flowers on the table for the German family that would replace his own. German army officers bragged openly about raping racially inferior Slavic women, a practice they called "virile methods." In a prison in Poznan, a headsman decapitated Poles with an axe. Later, in the interest of efficiency, the headsman was replaced by a guillotine.

In the western territories, Karski witnessed for the first time the German practice of "cleansing the lands" of Jews who were "intended . . . for destruction or removal." In the freezing streets of

Lublin, he came upon a public "gymnastics and hygiene lesson" in which Jews conducting forced exercises were beaten and taunted and doused with cold water by the Germans, who stripped the young boys naked and forced them to sing. In Warsaw, he saw a pregnant Jewish woman request a post-curfew pass, in case she went into labor in the night. The German functionary's response: "You don't need a pass. . . . Dogs are dying from hunger and misery, and you still want to give birth to Jews?"

Later, near Bełżec, he stumbled upon the beginnings of "a camp of Jews" who "walked and slept under the open sky" without adequate clothing:

> While one group slept, the other waited its turn, so that outer garments could be lent to one another. Those who waited jumped and ran around so as not to freeze. . . . All are frozen, in despair, unable to think, hungry—a herd of harassed beasts, not people. This has been going on for weeks.

*

It's not hard to imagine how these memories lived and burned inside him.

In the row houses.

At the hardware store.

In the classroom, at the School of Foreign Service at Georgetown University.

*

He smuggled these policeman's stories overland to the Polish government-in-exile in Paris. Carried them aboard the slow peasant trains to Kraków and Zakopane. Snow-skied them across Slovakia. By foot, by bus, by car. Hungary to Yugoslavia to Italy to France.

Before his report could be made official, one portion was

redacted. It was important that Karski report on the plight of the ethnic Poles, and it was fine that Karski report on the plight of the Jews, but it was too much for Karski to frankly assess the propensity among the rank and file of the Polish peasants to take pleasure because the Germans were finally teaching the Jews "a lesson."

He returned to Warsaw with bloodied feet. In his absence the Gestapo had busted the conspiracy of policemen, and his brother Marian languished in the new prison camp at Auschwitz. Soon he attempted the same route again, this time carrying an incriminating roll of microfilm. He didn't give his feet time to heal. It cost him badly. In a Slovakian mountain village, the pain in his ski boot forced him to stop for the night. Before morning, Karski and his guide were betrayed by the peasant who lodged them. The Gestapo torture and interrogation that followed left him with fewer teeth. Lying on a straw pallet in a tiny cell, in fear of breaking down and betraying secrets that might imperil his co-laborers in the Underground, Karski pulled a razor blade from a hiding place in the sole of his boot, slit his wrists, and lost consciousness as he bled out and waited to die.

He awakened strapped to a wooden table in a Slovakian hospital. A conspiracy of doctors, nuns, and nurses kept him safely out of prison, and then arranged for his transfer to a Polish hospital with lax security in Nowy Sącz by exploiting the Gestapo's desire to keep him alive long enough to talk. Karski feigned grave illness and asked for a priest to hear his confession and offer last rites. In the confessional, he gave the priest a name and address, and asked him to send for a cyanide capsule.

Under protest, the priest agreed. The Underground's local network was activated. A nurse brought the poison but begged him not to use it. A doctor sketched out an escape plan. It would happen at night. At the appointed hour, after the guards were drugged and sleeping, the doctor would stand in the doorway and light a cigarette. Karski would strip naked, walk the hallway, stop at the open window with the signal plant in the sill, climb out, and jump.

A group of rescuers from the Underground caught him as he fell. They threw clothes on his back, lifted him over the fence that separated the hospital grounds from the riverbank, hustled him onto a waiting rowboat, carried him piggyback down a country road, and hid him in a hayloft before first light.

The Gestapo pursued him relentlessly. Two Underground agents hid him beneath a pile of produce and smuggled him out of town in a horse-drawn cart. The Gestapo spent the rest of summer torturing and interrogating the people of Nowy Sącz. They imprisoned dozens they knew had no involvement in Karski's escape, simply to punish the town, to send a message. In the end, the rescuers were betrayed by one of their own, a young man who couldn't help bragging about his own heroism.

On the twenty-first of August, 1941, the Germans lined up thirty-two Poles in a brickyard.

A firing squad executed them with automatic rifles.

*

Thirty-two dead for this one alive.

Hammer in hand. Plaster in his hair.

Tall, thin bespectacled man at the front of the classroom.

Please take your seats. Open your textbooks to page forty-five.

*

His return to Warsaw and the Underground coincided with his brother Marian's release from Auschwitz because of a fortunate bureaucratic error. Their relationship had grown strained over Polish factional politics. The question of what the country would become after the war—how money would work, how it would be governed, and by whom—had always threatened to splinter the unity of the Underground. Karski's choice had long been to represent each party's message on its own individual terms to the government-in-exile, and to take sides never. To Marian, who had enlisted his brother in the first place, this choice had come to seem like a passive betrayal. Perhaps his brother was tipping the scales for the political opponents of the Pilsudskites, the authoritarian prewar faction to which Marian had belonged.

It is not hard to understand Marian's expectation of loyalty. Enough years separated them that Marian was almost as much a father figure as an older brother. He had been Karski's provider and protector. He had fed and sheltered him, employed him, provided him with false papers, trusted him with the secrets of the exiled government.

Now their roles were reversed. Marian had been stripped of his freedom, his profession, his secret powers. His release from Auschwitz had been a fluke. It seemed reversible. His only play was to lay low, try not to endanger himself or his wife, Jadwiga, be still, avoid attracting any predatory attention. But in Underground circles, his younger brother was a man on the rise. He'd suffered and escaped, served his quarantine, and now his proven skills as a near-invisible observer faced a historical opportunity.

*

One evening by candlelight in the unheated wreckage of a bombed building, Karski took a meeting with two of the few Jewish men in Warsaw who had not been sequestered by the Nazis to the Jewish Ghetto, and who smuggled themselves frequently in and out of the Ghetto through sewers and secret tunnels.

Leon Feiner and Menachem Kirschenbaum.

The two men were not natural allies. Feiner was an activist lawyer and leading member of the socialist General Jewish Labour Bund, and a fervent anti-Zionist who believed that Polish Jews were Poles, full participants in Polish politics whose duty was to stay in Poland and advocate for social and economic justice for all. Kirschenbaum was a leader of the General Zionists, a proponent of the notion that there would be no end to anti-Semitism in Europe, and that the only Jewish future lay in the establishment of a restored Jewish state in the ancestral homeland of Palestine.

Natural enemies in any other political context.

But understand the condition of the Warsaw Ghetto in August of 1942. It was surrounded by a wall nearly ten feet tall and topped with barbed wire. Escapees were shot on sight, for sport. Of the more than 450,000 Polish Jews who had been sequestered inside its walls, fewer than one-sixth remained. Disease was rampant. Already the Germans had administered an "artificial famine," and over 100,000 had died of starvation. Already the head of the Ghetto's Jewish governing council, Adam Czerniaków, had committed suicide after trying and failing to stop the deportation of 192 orphaned children to the Treblinka extermination camp. Each day 8,000–14,000 more were being "resettled" by cattle car to Treblinka, stripped, looted, and murdered with gas.

Feiner and Kirschenbaum had come to the end of themselves. (Karski later wrote that they "paced the floor violently, their shadows dancing in the weird light.") They had learned that the Underground was planning to send a young courier to London, to give a report to the government-in-exile and to leaders in the British government about the conditions of German occupation in Poland. They had summoned him, they said, because the world must know about what was happening to the Polish Jews, not only in the Warsaw Ghetto, but also throughout the country. And it was not enough, they said, to know what was happening to the Jews. It was necessary—morally imperative—that the Allied powers intervene immediately with a series of five "unprecedented steps."

1. The Allies must declare, among their primary war aims, the prevention of the extermination of the Jews.
2. The Allied propaganda arms must leaflet the German people to let them know about the genocide the Nazis had planned and were implementing.
3. The Allies must petition the German people to put a stop to the slaughter.
4. The Allies must inform the German people that if the slaughter did not stop, the German people would be held responsible.
5. Then the Allies must hold the German people responsible, by bombing German cultural sites and executing German prisoners of war who did not renounce Hitler.

The German people must be made to know, they told Karski, that the retaliatory bombing that would take place would not be "part of the military strategy," but that "this was done, and would continue to be done, because Jews are being exterminated in Poland."

"Gentlemen," Karski replied, "it is impossible. It is against international law. I know the British. They will not do it. It is hopeless. It weakens your case."

Kirschenbaum would not relent. It was Karski's moral responsibility to try.

"We are dying here!" he said. "Say it!"

*

At the end of the meeting, there was one last point about which Feiner pressed Karski. The British, he said, would not believe their story unless it was delivered by an eyewitness. Would Karski be willing to visit the Warsaw Ghetto?

Karski agreed.

They waited until a brief, six-day break in the Treblinka transports, while the Germans were preoccupied with sweeps in smaller towns. Feiner smuggled Karski through a cellar tunnel dug beneath an apartment building at 6 Muranowska Street that formed a portion of the outer wall of the Ghetto that separated Jewish Warsaw from Aryan Warsaw.

What he found there would haunt Karski for the rest of his life. Starving people walking glassy-eyed in the direction of nowhere. Dead bodies thrown naked into the street so their clothes could be used by the living, and so their families would not be forced to pay a German "burial tax." Emaciated children playing in the dirt. Pistol-toting German boys, members of the Hitler Youth, out on a "Jew hunt." When he tried to describe some of what he had seen in a late-life interview with Claude Lanzmann, who was then working on his authoritative nine-hour documentary *Shoah*, an impressionistic inarticulateness crept in. Watching the footage, one can see the emotional trauma of the memory begin to overwhelm Karski's long professorial habits of concrete speech, context, clarity:

> That odor. Children. Dirty. Lying . . . I saw a man with blank eyes, no word . . . The guide whispers, "He's just dying, he's just dying . . ." I saw some woman with a baby. Dead bodies lying on the street . . . "Remember. Remember." And I did remember . . .

*

A week later, Karski smuggled himself into the Ghetto again. He stayed longer. He met clandestinely with Jewish leaders, and refused—in proximity to so many starving people—the bread and water they offered as gestures of hospitality.

Still he had not seen enough, Feiner said.

The Ghetto was the Ghetto. Many had died in the Ghetto.

But beyond the Ghetto was something worse than the Ghetto.

*

Feiner sent him east, disguised as a Ukrainian guard, to the town of Izbica Lubelska, a "sorting" camp where the Nazis held Jews bound for extermination camps, looted their valuables, and told them they were being prepared for forced labor.

> I saw there one thousand, two thousand . . . Old, young, rabbis, children . . . Some were standing. Some were lying. The Germans were shooting . . . There was not enough room. So they were pushing the Jews. Mother did not want to give the child. The men would take the child by force. Putting this over their heads. Like a piece of meat . . .

The guards herded the people into boxcars they had painted with quicklime. They struck them with clubs and rifle butts. They bayoneted and shot those who were unable to move quickly enough. They filled the boxcars past capacity. Crushed protruding limbs as they slammed shut the iron doors.

*

We are dying here! Kirschenbaum had told him. *Say it!*

The time had come.

A written version of his official report, which included two pages about the Nazi atrocities against the Jews, was reproduced photographically on a tiny sliver of microfilm tucked and welded into a secret compartment inside a house key that Karski carried only as far as Paris. It was smuggled into London in a neutral country's diplomatic pouch a week ahead of his arrival. Karski carried his own eyewitness report in the more secure repository of his own mind and memory.

On the morning of his departure from Warsaw, Karski taped a vial of cyanide to the skin behind his scrotum. At the Cathedral of the Holy Cross, a priest placed a communion wafer in a locket and draped it with a chain around Karski's neck as a means of protection from harm, a gesture so moving that it caused Karski to return briefly to his apartment, rip the tape that bound the vial to the tender skin, and pour the poison down the sink.

Then he rushed to see the dentist, who injected him with a solution that caused his jaw to swell painlessly for the duration of his long train journey across the occupied territories of the Third Reich. His false papers indicated that he was a Frenchman heading home for a vacation from his work for the Germans at a Polish industrial plant, and the bandage around his swollen jaw prevented his Polish accent from giving him away.

*

It is not difficult to imagine that Karski arrived in London with high hopes. He had the microfilm. He had the conviction of the persuasiveness of his own eyewitness testimony. He had the diplomatic backing of the Polish government-in-exile. He had a full slate of meetings with officials of the British government and exiled leaders from among the Polish Jews. A report from the Bund, and another from the World Jewish Council in Geneva had preceded his own. It would have been reasonable to assume that each of these accounts would reinforce the veracity of the others, and that the monstrous crimes they revealed would stir the Allied powers to take quick and decisive action. And in the early days of Karski's London campaign, it did seem that these meetings might initiate such a movement.

On the strength of his testimony, Szmul Zygielbojm, one of two Jewish members of the exile Polish National Council, appealed directly to the British people, on the BBC:

> It will actually be a shame to go on living, to belong to the human race, if steps are not taken to halt the greatest crime in human history.

On December 17, 1942, British Foreign Secretary Anthony Eden read a joint statement by eleven Allied governments in the House of Commons, concerning "this bestial policy of cold-blooded extermination" and declaring that "those responsible for these crimes shall not escape retribution." A few minutes later, the entire House of Commons stood and observed a moment of silence for the Jews who had died at the hands of the Nazis.

These victories were merely symbolic. They were words. They were not even actionable words. They didn't come close to meeting Feiner's and Kirschenbaum's demands. There would be no declaration that the prevention of the extermination of the Jews would be among the Allies' primary war aims. There would be no leafleting of the German people concerning the genocide. There would be no retaliatory bombing of German cultural sites. There would be no threat of direct retaliation to the German people for their government's slaughter of the Jews. There would be no retaliatory execution of German prisoners of war who did not renounce Hitler.

And if these victories were merely symbolic, their symbolism was matched or exceeded by one exemplary defeat. After his meeting with Karski, the Catholic president-in-exile of Poland, Władysław Raczkiewicz, wrote a secret letter to Pope Pius XII, asking him to intervene. After all, Hitler himself was a baptized Catholic, as Karski had reminded his president.

The pope refused. He said he had already done all he could do for the Jews.

*

In Washington, as in London, Karski's testimony occasionally strained credulity in the eyes of government officials. Famously, at the end of Karski's meeting with Supreme Court Justice Felix Frankfurter, after Karski talked at great length about what he had seen in the Ghetto and the sorting camp, Frankfurter replied:

> Mr. Karski. A man like me talking to a man like you must be totally frank. So I must say: I am unable to believe you.

In response, perhaps, when Karski finally had the opportunity to meet with President Franklin D. Roosevelt in the White House, he muted his plea. He did not speak of his visits to the Ghetto or Izbica Lubelska. When he spoke of the Nazi concentration camps in Poland—Auschwitz, Treblinka, Belzec, Stanisławów, Dachau, Oranienburg, Mauthausen, Ravensbrück—he spoke of their primary inhabitants as Poles rather than as Jews.

But after he had established the scope of the Polish plight in general, he got specific about the Jews:

> The Germans want to ruin the Polish state as a state; they want to rule over a Polish people deprived of its elites. . . . With regard to the Jews, they want to devastate the biological substance of the Jewish nation.

As he had dozens of times before, in London, in Washington, he relayed the candlelight demands of Feiner and Kirschenbaum. Direct action. Intervention. Violent reprisal. Pain for the complicit citizens of the German state.

Otherwise, he told Roosevelt, the Jewish people of Poland "will cease to exist."

*

What was it like, to live with the knowledge of what happened next?

What was it like, to live with the knowledge of what did not happen?

*

An anecdote from E. Thomas Wood, one of Karski's biographers:

"Inevitably, when five o'clock came, he would look up, he didn't even have to look at his watch, he knew when it would be five, and he would say, Mr. Wood, this conversation is very interesting, but don't you think we ought to have a drink?"

*

For the rest of his life, the answer was always yes.

At five o'clock, a drink. Manhattan, easy on the vermouth.

Afterward, three days a week, an evening retreat from the work of the rehabilitation of the row houses to the life in the apartments he kept in the row houses.

For a time, he was not alone in this life.

In the early 1950s, Karski saw a woman dancing in a Washington synagogue. Her name was Pola Nireńska. An avant-garde artist and a Polish Jew. She had lost seventy members of her family, including most of her brothers and sisters, while she weathered the war in English. Karski courted her aggressively. By 1956 they were together at all times. By 1965, they were married.

And there was Marian and his wife, Jadwiga.

Immediate immigration to the United States was legally impossible, but Karski could get them as far as Paris.

For Marian, Paris was not far enough away from the possible reach of Stalin and the Soviets. According to Canadian law, anyone from a foreign country not otherwise qualified to immigrate could settle in Canada if they owned a farm and worked it themselves.

So Karski bought them a farm. Fifty acres near Montreal for Marian and Jadwiga. He paid for it with the last of his dwindling royalties from his 1944 memoir *Story of a Secret State*. By 1960, he had moved them to Washington, and afterward they moved along with him, partially renovated row house to partially renovated row house. Marian hated it. In Warsaw, their family had belonged to the social class that ran the country. Karski was a professor. This working-class labor—hammer and nail, plaster and wire—was beneath him.

But Karski didn't complain.

Work. Family. At five o'clock, a drink. In the evening, a retreat.

Such a life.

*

Karski's long silence ended in 1987—nine years after he was interviewed by Lanzmann, forty-three years after his appeals to the British, and forty-four years after he met with Roosevelt—when *Shoah* premiered for American audiences on public television, and Karski told his story publicly, in its fullness, for the first time since 1944.

The next morning, as he walked into his morning class at Georgetown, his students rose and began to applaud.

He received the applause with a mixture of gratitude and shame. He told Rabbi Harold White, a Georgetown colleague, that they were applauding a failure. He told Polish Minister of Foreign Affairs Władysław Bartoszewski, who as a member of the secret Jewish aid group Żegota contributed to an effort that saved the lives of several thousand Polish Jews: "You, Mr. Władysław, at least tried to save concrete people. You even managed to save some. Myself, I wanted to save millions, but I could not save anyone at all."

*

On May 11, 1943, Szmul Zygielbojm wrote a letter to the exiled president and prime minister of the Republic of Poland:

> By my death, I wish to give expression to my most profound protest against the inaction in which the world watches and permits the destruction of the Jewish people.

The next morning he took an overdose of sodium amytal and died.

On July 8, 1964, Marian Kozielewski, exiled policeman and farmer, beloved brother, committed suicide. Karski would care for his wife, Jadwiga, for the rest of her life.

On July 5, 1992, Karski's wife Pola Nireńska, who had earlier suffered from paranoid episodes while working on Holocaust-themed dance choreography, walked out onto the balcony of their eleventh-floor apartment and jumped to her death.

But Karski chose to live.

*

Lately I've been thinking about the humility of this choice. Six million disappeared against their will. How could he dishonor their memory by choosing his own death?

IV.
(ONE HUNDREN FIFTY-NINE DIGRESSIONS ON THE EPHEMERAL)

I'm here as a red light is in the street.

—Howard Finster

Junk Temples

1. The world is a disappointment.

2. The world is a disappointment, but there are means of escape. Doors to walk through. Secret doors, trapdoors, mystery doors. For example:

3. When I was a child, I began to hear music in color. *Here's a long song,* the deejay said. *The Beatles' "A Day in the Life."* (Toilet time. Cigarette time.) I saw:

4. Blue, magenta, white, orange. Out of silence, a final explosion of white.

5. A paradox: Memory's luminary color is a desaturated blue. In Joan Didion's *Blue Nights*, written in the wake of the death of a beloved daughter, the central mood recurs

alongside the evening hour the English call *the gloaming*, and the French call *l'heure bleue*: *the dwindling of the days, the inevitability of the fading, the dying of the brightness.* In William Gass's *On Being Blue*, amid blue talk and the blue erotic: *To be in the blue is to be isolated and alone.* In Maggie Nelson's *Bluets*, before the fading of the blue: *The half-circle of blinding turquoise is this love's primal scene.*

6. I want to digress using words into things that aren't words.

7. Things that aren't words radiate from the spines of the paperbacks on the shelves ahead of me. Shades of blue, orange, maize, yellow, cream, brown, magenta, lavender, lime, avocado . . .

8. At this moment, inside *l'heure bleue*, which is like a chamber of mirrors, I want to digress into numbers of subjects (2, 3, 5, 7, 11, 13, 17, 19, 23, 29, 31, 37, 41, 43 . . .). I've made a list:

9. Secret doors, trapdoors, mystery doors. Toilet time. Cigarette time. *The House of Breath.* In East Texas, the single tumbleweed. The voices of the fathers. Finster angels. The Tower of Babel. The gibbon moon. Dreams, visions, all things ephemeral. Balls of string obsessively wound and rewound. Susan Sontag. Jorie Graham. Henry Darger's *Realms of the Unreal.* Transcendence, escape. Junk temples. Ross Gay.

10. The way it feels when someone says: *What I really want is to*

disappear into you.

11. In any given *l'heure bleue*, it is difficult to abandon the idea of any particular other that one holds in one's head, in favor of the terrifying whole of the individual that is and is to become and be discovered.

12. I am tired of myself—

13. (the starfruit tree, the stolen teeth, the child with the axe, the East German Cold War hero who swam the River Spree three times in winter with her elderly relatives on her back so she could make her way to West Palm Beach, Florida, and ruin the lives of fifth-grade boys . . .)

14. —and want to digress into the lives of others.

15. A paradox: The self grows as the *self* recedes. The larger part becomes not what has *gone out*, so much as what has *come in*.

16. The literature of others. The language of others. The ideas of others. The films of others. The music of others. Generally speaking, the ghosts.

17. The ghosts have taken up residence in the house of memory. I do not want to revise them away. The problem is that they live together in a disorderly tangle. I can tell you the association of one to another, or I can juxtapose, but if I am true to the way they dye and deepen all things, I cannot make *narrative* of them. I cannot *please.*

18. And I do know how to please. How to place the gun on the mantel, plant the seed that will grow, shadow the fore. Find a key and sing. Wind the clock, pay the debt, unseal the skylight, weave and stack the modules, let the line that connects all things—the speaker's special logic—deliver the ending.

19. It is difficult to cast aside the voices of the fathers.

20. David Mamet: *Every scene should be able to answer three questions: 1) Who wants what? 2) What happens if [they] don't get it? 3) Why now?*

21. James Whitehead: *Clarity is the style of all honest men.*

22. Tom Petty: *Don't bore us. Get to the chorus.*

23. Raymond Carver: *No tricks.*

24. I am struggling with the practice of digression, which is the opposite of narrative.

25. Gilles Deleuze and Félix Guattari: *The two of us wrote* Anti-Oedipus *together. Since each of us was several, there was already quite a crowd.*

26. *A body without organs* is how they described the sequel. *A Thousand Plateaus.* A catalog of metaphors. A catalog of machines—*war machine, love machine, revolutionary machine*—against which the literary machine might be

measured. Instead of chapters: *Plateaus.* Instead of a single homogeneous reality: *Realms.* In a narrative, everything follows, even that which does not follow. In our broader experience of existence, everything is happening all at once. *Thought lags behind nature.*

27. A diagram of a tree: Below ground, a system of tiny roots that merge to become larger roots. At ground level, all the roots have merged to become the trunk of the tree. Closer to the sky, the trunk grows branches. The branches grow leaf buds. The buds become leaves. There is a hierarchy. The hierarchy brings order, *is* order. The order nourishes the parts, which create a pleasingly recognizable single organism. Look: a tree.

28. But there are other ways to be a tree.

29. Such as the eighty-thousand-year-old grove of quaking aspen in Utah's Fishlake National Forest. Forty-seven thousand trunk-and-branch stems covering over one hundred acres, but all of them nourished by a single network of roots. The grove, named Pando (Latin: *I spread*) is the largest organism by mass on our planet.

30. Deleuze and Guattari: *A system of this kind could be called a* rhizome.

31. *Bulbs and tubers are rhizomes. Plants with roots or radicles may be rhizomorphic in other respects altogether: the question is whether plant life in its specificity is not entirely rhizomatic.*

Even some animals are, in their pack form. Rats are rhizomes. Burrows are too, in all of their functions of shelter, supply, movement, evasion, and breakout. The rhizome itself assumes very diverse forms, from ramified surface extension in all directions to concretion into bulbs and tubers. When rats swarm over each other. The rhizome includes the best and the worst: potato and couchgrass, or the weed.

32. The day I first heard music in color, I felt as though a secret door had been opened to let the colors in. I was sitting on the drab white toilet, beside the drab white sink, the drab white door, three drab white walls, the drab white shower curtain that was beginning to yellow. Then, suddenly: Blue, magenta, white, orange . . .

33. For all my life I have been chasing the secret door.

34. I fell through a secret door this evening. On the television, as an orchestra plays John Williams's "The Imperial March," from *The Empire Strikes Back*, a flood of earliest memories: Being bathed in warm water. Crawling (swimming) a blue-carpeted floor. A boy hitting me in the head with a hammer. The explosion of blue, magenta, white, and orange into the drab white bathroom. The blue everywhere around Darth Vader from the first measure of strings and timpani.

35. Which was playing on my Fisher-Price record player, that day and every day of 1980, '81, '82, '83.

36. The Imperial March in Cigarette Time (inhale, exhale). Which is a hymn, a song of dark praise and religious devotion to a subordinate deity forged in fiery lava, left to die, and resurrected to rule by terror and supernatural force.

37. I want to show you the secret door, but the invitation is not mine to extend.

38. If you chase the secret door, you might find it. But more often it sneaks up on you, or opens under you, and you fall into it. Usually, when this happens, you are in a certain kind of posture, or in the presence of a certain kind of expression. In the shower, beneath the warm water. On a boat, at twilight. In meditation, in fasting, in prayer. Inside a story, a movie, a book. At the kitchen table, drawing. On a couch, playing the guitar while someone else plays the piano. On the interstate, at the arrival of a certain song.

39. You may fall into the secret door by your own means, but almost certainly someone else contributed to the creation of the secret door.

40. You may find the secret door at any age, but it is easier to find the secret door if you are a child.

41. A boy secretly plays the paper keys pasted to a cardboard piano in William Goyen's novel *The House of Breath*.

42. Mary Ruefle: *The words secret and sacred are siblings.*

43. As a child, Goyen lived in a pianoless house. His mother secretly cut the paper keys out of a newspaper ad and sent off a coupon for beginners' music lessons. *I straightaway devised Liszt-like concerti and romantic overtures,* an elderly Goyen remembered. *And so silent arts were mine: I began writing.*

44. Goyen conceived of *The House of Breath* as a series of arias, operatic set pieces featuring a single human voice. I know only one other person who has read it, a man who retired after working thirty-two years at a paper mill in Ohio to write Appalachian gothics lush with pills, lard, wigs, fish sticks, dead ants, orphans, murderers, and drifters "much welcome nowhere in the world."

45. Amidst the noise of the world, the operatic cry of a single human voice.

46. The retired mill worker let me borrow his copy of *The House of Breath.* This was the book, he said, that caused Goyen's wife, the actress Doris Roberts, to fall in love with him. He'd alchemized a lonely childhood in the tiny East Texas town of Trinity into a vast mythic space where the rain *turned half into snow and I was drenched and frozen; and walked upon a park that seemed like the very pasture of Hell where there were some couples whispering in the shadows, all in some plot to warm the world tonight, and I went into a public place and saw annunciations drawn and written on the walls.* Goyen insisted his new bride see the seed ground in the wild. So he drove her to East Texas. What she found there:

47. A tiny street. A house with a breezeway. In a coop somewhere a skinny chicken. The most uninspiringly ordinary place Roberts had ever seen. Rolling in a faint wind across the vast emptiness in front of them:

48. A single tumbleweed.

49. *Yet on the walls of my brain,* Goyen wrote, *frescoes: the kneeling balletic Angel holding a wand of vineleaves, announcing; the agony in the garden; two naked lovers turned out; and over the dome of my brain Creations and Damnations, Judgments, Hells and Paradises (we are carriers of lives and legends—who knows the unseen frescoes on the private walls of the skull?).*

50. Today I would like to retreat to 2 Lincoln Square, Columbus Avenue at West Sixty-Sixth Street in Manhattan, but the American Folk Art Museum is temporarily closed for design and gallery installations. The exhibit I want to see—*The Road to Heaven Is Paved by Good Works: The Art of Reverend Howard Finster*—hasn't been on display there, anyway, since January 5, 1990. Now it is night. Outside my window: a gibbous moon.

51. If you say *gibbous* moon, I think *gibbon* moon.

52. When I think of a gibbon moon I remember when my friend, who was studying the sexual proclivities of bonobos, volunteered to run naked through a forest at night for a film project we were too young to know how to land, and how

later we had a falling out over transportation to a wedding in Wisconsin, and when I regret that we never spoke again, the memory of his voice is bound up (ropes, chains) in the smell of burnt toast.

53. I forgot to say: *The House of Breath* proceeds mostly in creams and yellows.

54. Last night I had a dream that tasted like the withered arm of the kitchen chair in my grandmother's trailer beside the Frigidaire with the five green-and-yellow fish magnets made of ribbon, and on the steps behind the baptismal I couldn't save a friend from the church fire and the world in its terror was cream and yellow.

55. Today I would like to tell you the origin story of Howard Finster, the most famous folk artist in American history.

56. In Valley Head, Alabama, when Howard Finster was three years old, his dead sister Abbie Rose walked down from a secret door in the blue sky wearing a white gown and declared upon him a prophecy: "Howard, you're gonna be a man of visions."

57. Finster's father was a lumberjack. His mother, who was adept at making quilts, was a Christian, but his father was, in Finster's words, a sinner. As a child, Finster confessed his call to preach to a schoolteacher who was seated with the choir at a revival service at Lee's Chapel Baptist Church. The schoolteacher summoned the boy to the stage

to "confess his calling," and that was the evening Howard Finster preached his first sermon.

58. Let me confess to a temptation common to writers of fiction and nonfiction alike. Although it's true that history has not recorded the subject of Howard Finster's first sermon, I would like to invent one.

59. William Faulkner, in a letter to Malcolm Cowley: *I don't care much for facts, am not much interested in them, you can't stand a fact up, you've got to prop it up, and when you move to one side a little and look at it from that angle, it's not thick enough to cast a shadow in that direction.*

60. The subject of Howard Finster's first sermon was out of the eleventh chapter of the book of Genesis. The story of the Tower of Babel.

61. Not so long after Adam and Eve were expelled from the Garden of Eden, human beings began to multiply, but they were failing to fill the earth, as the Lord had instructed. The tribe of people mostly stayed together in the same place, and when they moved to a new place, they moved together. *Now the whole earth,* Genesis tells us, *had one language and the same words.*

62. This tribe—all the living descendants of Adam and Eve—migrated from the East, settled on a plain in the land of Shinar, and began an industrial-scale operation in the making of brick and mortar. Then they said:

63. *Come, let us build ourselves a city and a tower with its top in the heavens, and let us make a name for ourselves; otherwise we shall be scattered abroad upon the face of the whole earth.*

64. (Imagine the smell of revival three hours into the night service at the Lee's Chapel Baptist Church. The heat, the sweaty bodies, the mingling breath. Imagine the burnt orange humidity in the wooden pew. Imagine the child Finster, standing on the revival stage, pronouncing these words, which have around them the aura of cream and yellow.)

65. So the tribe of the descendants of Adam and Eve began to build their city and their tower to heaven, as the child Finster was saying. And when the Lord came down from the sky to see it, he said:

66. *Look, they are one people, and they have all one language, and this is only the beginning of what they will do; nothing that they propose to do will now be impossible for them. Come, let us go down and confuse their language there, so that they will not understand one another's speech.*

67. Here, perhaps, the child Finster got it wrong. Perhaps he had been told, as I as a child was told, that the Lord, in his anger, caused them to speak mutually unintelligible languages, scattered them by language group all over the face of the earth, and then, in a mighty coup de grâce to the prideful tribal monoculture, toppled the tower.

68. Imagine the rain of rubble at such a demolition. Rubble from the low places. Rubble from the heavens. A debris field as wide as the stratosphere is tall. Crushed buildings. Spontaneous fires. A city . . .

69. In ruin. In tatters.

70. Molly Peacock: *How else but in tatters should a world be?*

71. But that's not what happened. The tower was not destroyed. When the people were scattered by language to the four corners of the earth, the city was simply abandoned. The tower was abandoned. It was given the name Babel, because it was there that the Lord confused (in the ancient Hebrew: *balal*) the language of the people of the earth. As a memorial to the wrath of God, it stood.

72. For how many years did it stand? For some duration of time, it stood—in the year 2024 it is still remembered that the Tower of Babel did once stand—and then, gradually or suddenly, it ceased to stand.

73. And then it was gone.

74. This morning I read an interview with Jane Smiley, a novelist who originally trained to be a medievalist. *And when you are a medievalist, you don't study what's good, you study what's left. And you try to find good things in it. So you come to appreciate every fragment of every bit that's left. And try to glean something from that fragment, whatever it is.*

75. T. S. Eliot: *In the faint moonlight, the grass is singing.*

76. Sappho. "Fragment 105(a)," tr. Anita George

You: an Achilles' apple
Blushing sweet on a high branch
At the tip of the tallest tree.
You escaped those who would pluck
your fruit
Not that they didn't try. No,
They could not forget you
Poised beyond their reach.

77. Last night I dreamed again of the earthquake in Ouest Province. The mountainside buckled and deformed in sinusoidal waves and stayed that way. In the valley the concrete mausoleum graves cracked open, and the bones and bodies spilled out into the grass, and everything was wine like the ancient sea, and I lifted you there, your body from the grass, and for a second time I could not revive you, and before I awakened, I tore my hair from the roots.

78. For many years I had stopped dreaming of fire and graves broken open.

79. It is difficult to cast aside the voices of the fathers.

80. When I was a child, the traveling preachers said on the Day of the Lord the sky will turn blood red at dusk, and Christ will appear in the sky on a white horse, carrying a

sword, and he will point it to the earth, and the graves will crack open, and the dead in Christ will meet him in the air, first the dead and then the living, but those living who are left behind will face seven years of torment, and, child, you do not want to be left behind. So every day at dusk I waited at the window.

81. In West Palm Beach, Florida, the western sky turns blood red at the horizon for a half hour every day at dusk.

82. Some visions are trapdoors. Not all visions are.

83. Howard Finster: *Since i done this piece. Visions multiplied unbeli-evable. I. Could not draw all of them I make notes and sketch by hundreds I am now on this 4000 and 91 pieces of folk art since 1976 Jan-8. Years for you . . .*

84. The visions multiplied unbeli-evable. For Finster, the art was subordinate to the messages embedded in the visions. Although he had a conventional Southern Baptist notion of hell—brimstone, the Lake of Fire, eternal torment—he did not have the temperament to match. *I love all people,* he said. *Sinners are my favorite people because they are the people I would like to win for God. Since I don't condemn no kind of religion, I have all kinds of people to talk to.*

85. For Finster, the art was subordinate to the messages embedded in the visions, but he was wrong. When I go toward the visions of Howard Finster, I am looking for the secret door.

86. When I look at the Finster Angel, I hear . . .

87. *. . . the kneeling balletic Angel holding a wand of vineleaves, announcing; the agony in the garden; two naked lovers turned out; and over the dome of my brain Creations and Damnations, Judgments, Hells and Paradises . . .*

88. Wisława Szymborska: *In a split second the dream / piles before us mountains as stony / as real life.*

89. When I look at the Finster Angel, I see no tumbleweed. At the memory of the western sky red at the horizon, some heady return to the heightening that time and education have bled away. On the walls of my brain, frescoes.

90. Amidst the noise of the world, the operatic cry of a single human voice.

91. Per Barry Hannah: *Mr. Brain, he want a song.*

92. This evening I'm thinking again about transcendence, and how and why human beings seek it. Nearby, within arm's reach: a lit candle, a vinyl record on a turntable, a finger of single malt Scotch in a glass tumbler, but you're not here with me.

93. An ugly confession: Like Finster, I was raised among Southern Baptists. Like Finster, I was convinced at a very young age that I had a calling to preach. Unlike Finster, I went to school to study and prepare.

94. In my classes, I learned about the history of Christianity, its many fractures and schisms, the political processes through which the canon of Scripture, which I had previously been taught was breathed into the ears of the human scribes by the Spirit of God, was worked out by committees of powerful men who weren't always in agreement about what went in and what stayed out. I learned about the centuries-long, multiple-author process by which the existing books were accumulated. I learned about the competing source texts, the problems of translation from ancient languages, the often fantastical Apocryphal and deuterocanonical works that survive alongside the books I thought I knew, the contemporary scholarly debates that were coming to be known as the quest for the historical Jesus. In philosophy classes, I was learning about the logical fallacies—the appeals to authority, the appeals to emotion, the appeals to tradition, the circular reasoning—that had underpinned my understanding of almost everything.

95. A notion out of Jorie Graham: *You wanted to / have vision / but the gods / changed.*

96. Lawrence Weschler once told me about his afternoon lunch with the president of the Yugoslav War Crimes Tribunal in The Hague. All day, every day, the victims and perpetrators described murders, tortures, rapes, and mass killings in excruciating detail. Weschler asked the man how he kept himself sane while being "obliged to gaze into such an appalling abyss." The judge replied: "As often as possible, I make my way over to the Mauritshuis museum,

in the center of town, so as to spend a little time with the Vermeers."

97. As it happened, my university housed the Warner Sallman Collection, including Sallman's original oil paintings of Jesus, which were the dominant images of Jesus for American Protestant Christians beginning in 1940 because of the relentlessness of their marketing by the vulture capitalists Kriebel & Bates and the Gospel Trumpet Company. Certainly, they were the images that came to my mind when I imagined Jesus. I had seen the paintings—especially the ubiquitous *Head of Christ*, which has been reproduced for profit more than 500 million times—in church bulletins, on greeting cards, on the walls of churches, in the homes of friends, on the covers and endpapers of Bibles.

98. Weschler: *I had a sudden further intuition as to the true extent of Vermeer's achievement—something I hadn't fully grasped before. For, of course, when Vermeer was painting those images, which for us have become the very emblem of peacefulness and serenity, all Europe was Bosnia (or had only just recently ceased to be): awash in incredibly vicious wars of religious persecution and proto-nationalist formation, wars of an at-that-time unprecedented violence and cruelty, replete with sieges and famines and massacres and mass rapes, unspeakable tortures and wholesale devastation.*

99. In the gallery, as I studied Sallman's *Head of Christ*, a religion professor appeared at my elbow. I knew him; he

was my teacher. "What do you see in the painting?" he said. "Jesus," I said. "Which one?" he said.

100. I don't believe my teacher could have asked a more threatening question than *Which one?*, because my faith—my primary reason for making all the life-shaping choices I was making—was predicated on a notion out of the book of Hebrews: *Jesus Christ is the same yesterday today and forever. Do not be led away by diverse and strange teachings.*

101. He gave me a book. *Jesus Through the Centuries*, by the Yale historian Jaroslav Pelikan, who intended "not a life of Jesus . . . but a series of images portraying his place in the history of culture."

102. In the first century, for the Jews who were his contemporaries, he was Jesus the Rabbi, the teacher and prophet whose Jewishness permeated the New Testament. For the Christian missionaries of the Greco-Roman world of the second and third centuries, he was Jesus, the Light of the Gentiles. By the fourth century, at the birth of the "Christian Empire," with Constantine on the Roman throne, he was Jesus, King of Kings.

103. And so on, for two thousand years, each historical place and time imagining the Jesus that best fit their cultural need. There was a Jesus to bolster the powerful and a Jesus to console the powerless: the Cosmic Christ, the Son of Man, the Monk Who Rules the World, the Bridegroom of the Soul, the Universal man, the Prince of Peace, the

Teacher of Common Sense, the Poet of the Spirit, the Liberator, the Man Who Belongs to the World.

104. In the gallery again, alone this time, studying Warner Sallman's *Head of Christ*, the hard question: "Which one?" A year or two later, I knew what the answer was not: Supernatural Lord and Savior. An occupational hazard, to be sure, because by then I was standing on a stage at a church, and the language of my job description included the phrase: *discerning and clarifying the vision* . . .

105. *You wanted to / have vision / but the gods / changed.*

106. This evening I'm thinking again, soberly, about transcendence, but in those waning days of standing on a stage at a church, I was obsessed with the question of what was not happening when I walked through the back door of the sacred space and in good faith raised my prayers, my intentions, my arms to the sky.

107. The sky, which did not open. The heart, which did not speed. But there were other doors.

108. Eighteen other doors, each of which led to a different dark room in the same building in Jupiter, Florida. A lucky thing: 1999 was a good year for movies. *Magnolia*, *Being John Malkovich*, *Girl, Interrupted*, *Fight Club*, *American Beauty*, *The Matrix*, *The Sixth Sense*, *Eyes Wide Shut*, *Election*, *The Virgin Suicides*, *Boys Don't Cry*, *The Iron Giant*, *The General's Daughter*, *The Cider House Rules*, *The Insider*,

Three Kings, Titus, Stigmata, The Straight Story, Limbo, The Limey, The Hurricane . . .

109. Another lucky thing: The new movies came out on Friday, my day off. Every Friday, I holed up in the movie theater, five movies noon to midnight. With gratitude and great happiness I bought a ticket for every one. In the theater darkness, the sky did open. The heart did speed. The light flickered above our heads, but not all the colors proceeded from the projector.

110. Frank Stanford: *I am not asleep, but I see / a limb, the fingers of death, the ghost / of an anonymous painter / leaving the prints of death / on the wall; the bright feathers . . .*

111. Last night I dreamed there was a fire in the theater where we watched the forbidden films in secret. In the smoke I lost you. I searched and searched but I could not find you.

112. Mary Ruefle: *The words secret and sacred are siblings.*

113. In recent years I have come to delineate between two kinds of literature. There is the perfunctory and there is the secret door. The line that separates them is drawn not by race, class, gender, genre, aesthetic position, historical time and place, or moral or ideological rightness. It is noticeable, instead, by a discernible but difficult-to-define quality that David Foster Wallace called "the click."

114. If you hear the click, you've found the secret door.

115. A good first sentence for a memoir: *For all my life I have been chasing the secret door.*

116. Q: How will I know if I have passed through the secret door? A: You will see an aura of color.

117. This afternoon I'm thinking about the Catholic hospital janitor Henry Darger, a graduate of the Lincoln County Asylum for Feeble-Minded Children who spent over fifty of his years alone in a rented room in Wicker Park, Chicago, secretly creating the fifteen-thousand-page illustrated epic he called *The Story of the Vivian Girls, in What is Known as the Realms of the Unreal, of the Glandeco-Angelinian War Storm, Caused by the Child Slave Rebellion.*

118. A representative page from Darger's epic:

119. Some mysteries concerning Darger's epic:

120. Why do all the little girls, when unclothed, have penises? Did Darger not know that most little girls are born without them? Why, for heroine-avengers, seven child princesses? Why do these princesses so closely resemble the cartoon children of catalog advertisements contemporary to Darger's early life? Why are the adults so sadistic? Why is it that the creatures who aid and protect the children are hideous dragons? What does it mean that our own earth orbits the planet of the Realms of the Unreal as a moon? From the vantage point of the Realms of the Unreal, what can be known about our planet that we cannot see because

we see from too close-up? Of the two competing endings, which is the true culmination of the Unreal, the one in which the princesses, the Vivian girls, prevail, or the one in which they are slain by the child slavers they have spent fifteen thousand pages battling? Are the two endings truly in competition? Are they meant to sit side by side, not indeterminately, but rather in eternal tension, because in his realm as in ours, the battle remains unresolved for the duration? Was Darger simply unable to decide the outcome for himself? Or, in an act of prophetic faith, did he leave the outcome to be decided by whomever discovered the manuscript he left behind?

121. Some mysteries concerning Darger's life:

122. Was he complicit at the age of twenty, as some historians have speculated but few believe, in the kidnapping and murder by asphyxiation of the child Elsie Paroubek in the spring of 1911? If not, what was it about her case that caused him to fixate upon it for the rest of his life, to use it as an informing source for *The Vivian Girls*, in which children who are kidnapped and abused by adults are saved by rescue squads made up of other children? When Darger thought of Elsie Paroubek, did he feel guilty that she was taken in his city and yet he could not save her? Or was his obsession a function of an enormous empathy: When Darger thought of Elsie Paroubek, did he see a suffering akin to his own?

123. Did Darger learn about Elsie Paroubek from the

sensational accounts in the *Chicago Daily News*? If so, what was it about her story that so called to him that after he lost the newspaper clipping that included the child's picture, he spent the next fifty years fretting about its loss, writing about it in his diary, reproducing her face from memory in his *Vivian Girls* illustrations?

124. Or did Darger briefly know Elsie Paroubek? Had he met her in passing, at the market or in the street? Had she smiled at him as an act of innocent kindness? Had she once taken his hand and pulled him toward something she wanted to show him? Did she once speak to him as though he might be more fellow traveler than graduate of the Lincoln County Asylum for Feeble-Minded Children? In all of his life, did anyone ever say to Henry Darger the words *I love you*?

125. Robert Creeley: *It is hard going to the door / cut so small in the wall where / the vision which echoes loneliness / brings a scene of wild flowers in a wood.*

126. The man-child Darger bent over watercolors, tracing paper, newspapers and magazines, the memory of a person half-known now gone, the vision which echoes loneliness, the avenging dragon, the battle unresolved for the duration, the light that flickered above our heads, the aura of cream and yellow under the gibbon moon which is our own earth . . .

127. Amidst the noise of the world, the operatic cry of a single human voice.

128. But I forgot to say: The means of escape and the means of entrapment sit side by side.

129. Olivia Laing: *One of the strangest items I'd come across in [Darger's] archive was a medium-sized notebook which had been labelled* Predictions, June 1911 – December 1917. *It looked like an account book, with vertical pink columns filled with a tiny, cramped hand. As I deciphered the entries, I realized it represented an attempt to bargain with God, to make desired events take place in the real world by threatening violence against the Christian Angelinian forces in the Realms of the Unreal. These threats mostly concerned lost manuscripts and pictures, which if not returned would be avenged by dreadful losses in Darger's imaginary war.*

130. And I forgot to tell you about all the other things Henry Darger left behind in his room of secrets. The hoard. Discarded eyeglasses plucked from the Chicago streets. Steamer trunks filled with empty Pepto-Bismol bottles, ancient coloring books, the balls of string he obsessively wound and rewound . . .

131. And I forgot to tell you about the other hoarders. The antique trader Stephen Cary Blumberg, who emerged unbathed from his seventeen-room house in Ottumwa, Iowa, carrying a leather pouch of gold coins in his underwear, to burglarize rare books collections at libraries—perhaps as much as $662,000 worth from the University of Oregon library alone—and bring them home to live alongside his collections of pioneer letters, railroad records, the balls

of string he obsessively wound and rewound, Victorian glass doorknobs, and the skins of garter snakes. Or the paranoid turn-of-the-century society widow Ida Mayfield Wood, who retreated unbathed for twenty-five years into two Herald Square Hotel rooms filled with empty cracker boxes, stacks of yellowed newspapers, stacks of old wrapping papers, and fifty-four trunks stuffed full with bolts of European lace, designer gowns, tiaras, gifts from American presidents, letters from luminaries such as Charles Dickens, priceless watches, gem-encrusted bracelets, and the balls of string she obsessively wound and rewound, and where upon her death her sister found $1 million in cash hidden in pots and pans and shoeboxes and secret oilcloth pockets inside her nightgowns and dresses, and a $40,000 diamond necklace hidden in a Cracker Jack box. Or the Collyer brothers, Homer and Langley, of 2078 Fifth Avenue, Manhattan, whose iron-barred house was so full of junk—newspapers, balls of string obsessively wound and rewound, boxes, chairs, pianos, an X-ray machine, 120 tons in all, piled floor to ceiling—that it took police five hours to find ten-hours-dead Homer's body (starvation, heart attack), and another three weeks fighting through booby traps, mazes, and hollowed-out nests, to find five-weeks-dead Langley's body, which lay inside a two-foot-wide tunnel of drawers and bed springs, crushed by one of his own booby traps.

132. Jane Kenyon: *I am the blossom pressed in a book, / found again after two hundred years . . .*

133. And I forgot to tell you about Paradise Garden, where Howard Finster brought his junk.

134. Broken glass, slabs of concrete, rusty hubcaps, broken mirrors, bicycle parts, an abandoned Cadillac . . .

135. 1961. For sale: Two and a half acres of swampland north of Summerville, Georgia, half a mile from where the state would build Hays State Prison, and Finster bought them. He spent seven years filling the muck with dirt. He found three springs on the property and rerouted them. He killed over one hundred snakes. The one time he was bitten, he drained the bite by sucking it, then went back to work. He planted beds of flowers in the branches of the springs.

136. The flowers grew year-round out of the abundance of water.

137. Finster: *I started going to the dump and collecting old broken dishes and molding bricks. You name any valuable thing that is of benefit to the human race and you are naming something that is being wasted every day in our country. I'd find some of the prettiest things you've ever seen. Sometimes twenty-two-carat gold dishes would be broke and thrown in there. I always wanted to build something like a city. When I was a small boy I'd take rocks and line 'em up and have streets and a little town.*

138. He began building a concrete walkway. He molded in gold watches, gold rings, jewelry, diamonds, *anything that shined*. Purple milk bottles. Fragments of mirrors. He

put up walls. Buildings. Art studios. A bicycle and lawn mower repair workshop. A woodshop. A recording studio. Animal pens. A dog pen. A pigeon sanctuary. A solar room. A rabbit hutch.

139. As late as 1976, Finster was still subsidizing the building operation by fixing bicycles and lawn mowers. One afternoon he was patching a scratched chassis with white paint. He dipped his finger into the bucket, and when he pulled the finger away, a face formed in the paint, and he heard a message of instruction in the vision: *Paint sacred art.* A few months later, a fifteen-foot-tall man with a *face wide as a Frigidaire* appeared at his garden gate with a new message: *Howard, get on the altar.* Then he shrunk to normal size and walked away.

140. For four days, Finster pondered this vision. On the fifth day, a family arrived at the front door, asking Finster to perform their father's funeral. They brought a picture of the dead man. When Finster looked at the picture, he realized he was looking at the face of the fifteen-foot-tall man. At the funeral, he told the mourners of this second vision, and as he spoke, its meaning was revealed to him. He must close down his repair business and paint sacred art full-time. So he did. He abandoned his tools forever, and molded them into the concrete walkway so he could never use them again.

141. He painted on scraps of wood. He painted the walls. He painted the Cadillac. At the dump he found an oxen yoke

and painted on the yoke beam the words of Christ from the eleventh chapter of Matthew: *Take my yoke upon you.* He made sculptures out of concrete and molded them to the walls. He made standalone sculptures. A serpent. A giant foot. A Coin Man with money molded into his chest. A Honeycomb Mountain made with paper horns and discarded Pringles potato chip cans for molds. A surgeon gave him a jar that held a little boy's tonsils, and he molded that into a wall. A coroner brought him the body of an unknown girl of seventeen who had been killed during the Civil War, and Finster built an Egyptian tomb for her bones covered by a glass top through which you could see her teeth. He tried to sell his leftover bicycle and lawn mower parts for scrap metal, but he wasn't happy with the offered price. So he built them into a thirty-foot steel tower wrapped around his living fruit trees, encircled by artichokes, butterbeans, and wild roses, with a loft for birds and a subterranean den for field snakes.

142. His paintings began to sell. The buyers included the Library of Congress and the Smithsonian American Art Museum, and eventually the Harvard Art Museums, the National Portrait Gallery, the Whitney, actors and musicians such as Robin Williams, Michael Stipe, and David Byrne. Finster used the money to buy more adjacent land. An abandoned church with a sway in the roof stood on the lot behind Finster's. He had a vision to put a dome on top to hide the sway. He made the dome thirty feet wide through the first layer. Twenty-seven through the second. Twenty-five through the third. Each level had sixteen sides. He

cut every angle with two measuring sticks, no ruler. He squared to the top of the studs. The columns were of his own design, cut at odd angles beneath a stacked steeple. At the top of the steeple, he built a mirror-encrusted spire, and capped it with a copper toilet ballcock.

143. A handmade temple to the sky. The World's Folk Art Church. A junk collage. For how many more years will it stand?

144. Last year I read—or thought I read—a biography of Susan Sontag, or a memoir about Susan Sontag, or an essay or a book by Susan Sontag, and in it was the phrase "junk temples."

145. But today, and yesterday, and the day before, I have been searching the library databases. I have scrutinized indexes, and I have reread whole books. I have consulted critical volumes. I have googled. And I can find no evidence, nothing to link Susan Sontag to the phrase "junk temples."

146. And yet as it rattles half-formed inside me—

147. junk temples

148. —something forms alongside and around it, photon and electromagnetic wave, an aura of cream and yellow. It goes something like this:

149. All temples are made of material that was not temple

material until it was joined to the temple. Eventually all temples fall. When temples fall, the material that remains is no longer temple material. It is junk, to be recycled, or hauled and dumped, or left to rot in place. What makes a temple a temple? All temples derive their templeness from the esteem of those who deem them temples. Special architecture is not required. Only esteem is required. These secular days, in the absence of adequate temples, one may seek a temple. The act of seeking and finding can make a temple of anything anyone has made. Seeking in a posture of openness. Seeking in a posture of forgetting. In a library. In the shower. In a concert hall. In a darkened theater. On the toilet. Good temples, bad temples, as time will reveal. The temple that enlightens and the temple that destroys. The temple that wastes time, and the temple that makes time redeemable. Temples high and low, but we may not agree which is which. The temple which is was once the temple which is not, and the temple which is will one day be the temple which is not. *From dust you came and to dust you shall return.*

150. All temples are junk temples.

151. Doesn't every secret door proceed from a junk temple? In sixty, seventy, eighty years of life, how much it is possible to understand about nature and our place in it? The nature of our species. The nature of physics, of the workings of things so large or so small that they are beyond our ability to perceive. The nature of perception itself, of consciousness, of time. In any given *l'heure bleue*, thought

lags behind nature. In any given ruins, among the rubble, a fragment, a song, a disappearing song, the only song we have. *In the faint moonlight, the grass is singing . . .*

152. William Butler Yeats: *I pace upon the battlements and stare / On the foundations of a house, or where / Tree, like a sooty finger, starts from the earth.*

153. If the idea of junk temples proceeded from the mouth or writing hands of Susan Sontag, and if it is now irretrievable to me in its original form, bearing its original meaning, then let it become a metaphor for itself and thereby a metaphor for all things, as all things are indeed moving in the direction of the irretrievable.

154. If I am afraid that one day I will forget your face, I know with assurance that one day you will forget mine, as I know with assurance that one day all our faces will be forgotten, as I know with assurance that one day the concept of forgetting will likewise be forgotten, and when I think these thoughts, something forms alongside and around them, photon and electromagnetic wave, an aura of cream and yellow.

155. The English language is going away. Also: Swahili, Mandarin, Quechua, Hungarian. Also: the sky, the stars, the sun, the earth.

156. James Laughlin: *Last night you came into my / dreams as wild as a bird that / has flown in an open window.*

157. When you are not here with me your face fades from my memory and I fight, claw, shelter, swim against the fire, wind, rain, and sea to retrieve it. This evening my typing hands build a monument to it. But the statue stands still while the person proceeds, and the night is approaching, and you are not here with me.

158. . . . *in a split second the dream / piles before us mountains as stony / as real life* . . .

159. Ross Gay: . . . *because we all know the tongue's clumsy thudding / makes of miracles anecdotes let me stop here* . . .

V.
(THREE SPECIMENS, A DIAGNOSIS, AN EXHORTATION)

Every closet's been examined.
Every shelf has been explored.

—Wisława Szymborska

The Sickness and the Song

I.

Once upon a time in 1968, there were nine sailors.

Their task was to circumnavigate the globe without stopping, British port to British port. Along the way: the Atlantic, the Cape of Good Hope, the Indian Ocean, the Roaring Forties, the route south of Australia and New Zealand, Cape Horn, the Atlantic again, up the coast of South America, north and east across the North Atlantic, home. Whoever arrived first would receive a trophy called the Golden Globe.

Seven were accomplished sailors; two were amateurs. Eight were well-funded; one was leveraged to the hilt. Four turned back before leaving the Atlantic Ocean. The fifth turned back at the Cape of Good Hope. The sixth sank 1,100 nautical miles from shore. The seventh committed suicide. The eighth sailor won the race.

The ninth sailor could have won the race. Although he set sail eighty-four days later than the first sailor, his yacht was the first to be seen from the Falkland Islands, the last major waypost before the race turned northward toward the finish line at England's southern shore. The French navy was already waiting offshore to escort him there. Newspapers on four continents made predictions about the date of his arrival. Already the world was beginning to know his name.

Bernard Moitessier.

He had made a conspirator of everything. The wind, the rain, the sea.

But he no longer cared about the race.

As he rounded the tip of South America, there were no icebergs. The yacht was moving at a steady clip, but he did not turn north. He kept sailing east. When the water turned calm, he put on his wetsuit and dove underwater with a putty knife to scrape the gooseneck barnacles from the hull bottom.

He kept a journal. His thoughts on Tasmania. The feeding habits of sharks. The porpoises of the South Pacific and the penguins of Galápagos. Europe was a snake pit. He planned to seek the island of Tahiti in the trade winds. Fish soup became blood and warmth within him. The color of blood was the color of life. The sunset past the Cape of Good Hope was the color of blood.

His hair had grown long and tangled. More than once the gale winds knocked the yacht down. Somewhere escort seagulls led all boats to land, but now the seagulls were far away. The only sound was the sound of the water. The long streaks of foam. At dawn the sky turned white above them. All other boats were far away. All other people. Time itself was receding. He was free.

Ten years ago I started reading this story thirty-six thousand feet above Memphis, Tennessee, in a book I bought at a Hudson

Booksellers in the Atlanta airport. I turned the second-to-last page as the plane landed in Salt Lake City, and the last page in the shadow of the Wasatch Mountains, in a van full of children whose father had invited me to Provo. I thought about it all the way to Provo, and I haven't stopped thinking about it ever since.

Bernard Moitessier, the sailor who quit the race because he simply wanted to sail the seas.

For the last ten years I've been thinking about him all the time.

II.

I used to own four or five thousand books.

These books had become a burden. Not just because I had to find a place to shelve or store them, and not just because they made more difficult the job of moving from one house to another.

The problem was that the books were everywhere. All over the house. Floor-to-ceiling. I had to look at them all the time. When I looked at them, what I saw was failure. I had spent most of the years of my twenties and thirties reading them, trying to rewire my brain. I had read mostly every page of every one of them. Very few were the pages I had not read.

What did I want from these books?

*

The ugly fact, Cormac McCarthy said, *is that books are made out of books.*

*

Out of these four or five thousand books, I had made two modest books of short stories. I had tried to make many more—novels, memoirs, essays, a hundred-page poem—but only the two books of stories had stuck. I had come to believe that the first one, which almost no one read, was not very good, except for one very long story loosely based on the life of my grandmother. Loosely, because I gave the woman in my story a much better life than my grandmother's. Unlike my grandmother, the woman in my story was married to a man who was kind to her, who cared for her, who really loved her.

I don't mean to say that this story was a nice story. It was very dark. It ended with the death in the bathtub of a senile woman who believes that her loving son, who is trying to bathe her, is really her childhood tormenter who beat his own little brother to death in a tobacco field and left the body to a pack of wild dogs. I'm glad none of these things happened to my grandmother.

But in another way, the story was a wish-fulfillment fantasy. If the beginning of life and the end of life are not good, it might be beyond anyone's ability to do anything about it, because our lives in those fragile stages are so often beyond our control. But what if, in between the bad, we could seize the middle? Isn't the middle, if we live long enough, the most of it? And what if, for whatever reason—fate, circumstance, the impositions of others, our own choices, our own failures—we couldn't seize the middle? Could a story—not a cheap story, something real, something as wild and unlikely as life itself—redeem the middle? Redeem the whole? Peel off a little piece somewhere?

What if, I thought, we could rewrite our lives and the lives of the people we love, replace some of the bad parts with good parts, balance out the pain?

*

I built the second book out of this idea. Sure, when we lived on earth everything was as bad as it was. But what if we spent eternity rewriting it until we could make it better?

I was thinking, for example, of my uncle, who had killed

himself twenty-something years into a truly terrible run that began with a brain injury when he was hit by a city dump truck. When you're meditating on those kinds of things, you're always chasing the cause-and-effect chain backwards, asking the question: Where is the moment in which, if I could create a small change, things would've been different? In other words: When did this story's trouble begin?

Around this time I was reading James Michener's *Hawaii*, an old mass market paperback pop novel that no one I knew would be caught dead reading. But right from the first page, I knew Michener was chasing the cause-and-effect chain backwards, asking the same question I was asking: When did this story's trouble begin?

Millions upon millions of years ago, the novel began, *when the continents were already formed and the principal features of the earth had been decided, there existed, then as now, one aspect of the world that dwarfed all others. It was a mighty ocean, resting uneasily to the east of the largest continent, a restless ever-changing, gigantic body of water that would later be described as pacific.*

Michener's logic was clear: If the subject is the trouble of Hawaii, the origin of that trouble—the point of no return, cause-and-effect-wise—can be found many millions of years ago, on the ocean floor, where the volcanoes are gearing up to spew the lava that will become the landmass of Hawaii.

And so it is, I realized, with all stories. If I was thinking about the poverty into which my uncle was born and raised in trailer parks throughout Florida as a prerequisite cause for the blue-collar employment that put him in the line of danger with the city dump truck that damaged his brain and ruined his chance to live the life he had planned and desired, then I was thinking about the people who had raised his parents in Kentucky, their parents and their parents' parents, the boat that had brought them from Europe, the shifting winds that had caused the English to defeat the Spanish Armada in 1588, the triumph of *Homo sapiens* over the Neanderthals, the origin of the universe.

*

The second book was a synthesis of this idea with the older idea of Flannery O'Connor's that had animated the first book:

The fact is that anybody who has survived his childhood has enough information about life to last him the rest of his days. If you can't make something out of a little experience, you probably won't be able to make it out of a lot.

In some small way, it worked. I came to think of the second book as "the little book that could." It sold pretty well for a collection of short stories from a small press. It was reviewed far and wide, mostly positively, occasionally glowingly. It kept me on the road for five months, reading and speaking at universities, bookstores, and salons, usually getting paid for my time. It helped me land, at the age of thirty-seven, a decent-paying job for the first time in my life, teaching at a university in Indianapolis.

*

The life of a writer, as seen on television, is full of problems.

You might, for example, be forced to decide whether you want to spend the winter in Manhattan or the Hamptons. If you stay in Manhattan, it might be hard to get any work done. There will be parties. You will be expected to attend, and drink, and smile and talk with people you secretly hate, who also secretly hate you. But if you stay in the Hamptons, you won't be able to visit the paintings at the art gallery from which your work draws its sustenance. And you might miss the season's performance of *The Magic Flute* at the Metropolitan Opera. You're staring down a winter, understand, without the arrival of the Queen of the Night.

These problems were not my problems.

When five months of modest success came my way, I was broke and sort of homeless. I owned a house in Toledo, Ohio. (Or, I would own the house, I supposed, once I had made the thirty years of payments I had promised the bank that held the mortgage.) My family lived there. It would take a while to sell. My kids had a favorable school situation. They needed to stay at least another year. To take the new job, this good, seemingly stable entry-level thing I had been working toward for fifteen years, I needed to be in Indianapolis at least the two days a week I met my classes. To tend the book tour, I had to spend, usually, two or three days a week flying to the East Coast, the West Coast, Chicago, Texas.

There wasn't enough money. More was coming in than before, but not enough to keep houses in two cities. Not enough to fund the book tour, not the way I planned to do it. There was debt. Student loans, credit cards, fuel and food bills rung up from the year before, which I had spent driving sixteen-hour round trips between my low-paid contingent teaching gig in Ohio and one last run I couldn't afford at graduate school in Iowa. That commuting year I rented a three-hundred-dollar-a-month room in Iowa City from a woman who refused to set the thermostat above sixty degrees in a season of negative twenty, thirty, forty wind chill advisories. I slept there when I could, but I wasn't always able, because I always had to rush back to Ohio to teach an eight o'clock class. Occasionally I splurged on a cheap hotel room. One night I slept in an elevator car. I learned how to sleep an hour or two in my rusty brown Toyota Camry in the winter at the Iowa 80 truck stop or in the parking lot of a Dunkin' Donuts in suburban Chicago.

Now, in Indianapolis, I put these skills to work. I slept where I could. In the car, in a thirty-dollar motel room, in a friend's attic, in an empty dormitory room at my old college, in a quiet study room on the second floor of a twenty-four-hour library, in a chair in a twenty-four-hour laundromat while my clothes were drying, in a twenty-four-hour gym, beneath the pews of a church sanctuary, and once or twice, fearful but lacking an alternative during a whiteout blizzard, in my new office. But mostly in the car. Blackout shades on the windows. Four layers of winter clothing. Insulated blanket. If there was enough gas I ran the engine all night, the sunroof cracked open to air away the demons of carbon monoxide.

*

The worst thing about sleeping in the car is the worrying. You're waiting for the knock on the window, which could be anyone. A would-be Good Samaritan (*Excuse me, sir, but do you have a safe place to sleep this evening?*) A would-be carjacker (*Open the goddamn door, motherfucker.*) A smug, self-appointed custodian of the business that controls the parking lot (*Listen, chief, you can't sleep here.*) Worst of all, a cop (*Step outside the car, please. License and registration. Do you mind if I have a look around this back seat? Have you been drinking?*)

So that's Sunday night, let's say. You set the alarm for four thirty, because you want to be out of the Lawrence Branch Library parking lot before the librarian arrives scared at five because you're ominously present. So you wake at four thirty. Your mouth tastes like old dirty pennies. Your throat is sore, and the windows are fogged up from your sour breath. The odometer says 298,912 miles. The digital thermostat on the sunroof console says Fahrenheit, eight degrees. You're hungry, and your arms are sticky. If you're lucky, you only have to pee. If not, the polite words for what you need to do—eliminate, evacuate, excrete, expel—do not apply. What you need to do is take an unpleasant shit, but for the next hour there is nowhere for you to go to deliver it.

You drive downtown and wait outside the natatorium. Your membership is a good investment. Seventy-five bucks a month for a heated building, a locker room, a shower, clean toilets, lap privileges in the enormous pool where they hold the US Olympic Trials.

At five thirty the natatorium doors open. You shit. You shower. You're too tired to swim. You shave, dress, brush your teeth. You unrumple some bills and stuff them into the black mouths of two vending machines. Orange Gatorade and a pack of Keebler cheese and peanut butter crackers. Breakfast.

At six o'clock the doors to your office building unlock automatically. Upstairs, in a tiny, windowless fifth-floor office that used to be a supply closet, you prepare to teach short stories by James Baldwin and Lorrie Moore. (*But these stories won't be taught,* you say out loud. *No matter what you say, they willfully do what they already do.*) At nine o'clock you observe a colleague's class. He tells the room that Cormac McCarthy isn't literature, then reads a poem by a nineteenth-century traveling salesman who made his first fortune telling crowds that his lifelong blindness had been cured by the tonic he held in his hands.

Around noon you close your office door and fall asleep at your desk. A knock on the door wakes you ten minutes later. Across the hall, the printer is broken. The face at the door wants to know if you know how to fix it. You try. When you are done trying, it is time to teach. When you are done teaching, it is time to drive to the airport and board the plane for Washington, DC.

When you land, the graduate student who picks you up is very nervous. On the drive to her suburban campus, on a freeway twelve lanes wide, she tells you she has a heart condition so severe that she could drop dead any minute. Forty-five minutes later, when she drops you off in front of a campus building, there is no one to greet you. Your itinerary says your hotel is a half mile away. You walk there, but when you arrive, your reservation has been misplaced. You don't know, in fact, who has made your reservation, but you do know that you are expected someplace for late-night drinks.

You wait with your bags in the lobby of a luxurious hotel. Eventually a frazzled assistant professor shows up in an actual tweed jacket with elbow patches. He straightens things out. You'll have a room for the night, but it won't be ready for an hour. *Would you like to store your bags in the luggage room?* The desk clerk points to an unattended open space across the lobby. Against the objections of your host, you bring your bags with you to his car.

The people you meet at the bar—more hosts—are grumpy. You are late, and you are mostly obligation, one out-of-town writer among four or five who will read for an audience at this week's literary festival. They seem not to be able to remember your name. You know some of their names, but you haven't read any of their books. You're not sure anyone has. They are the sort of people who are known as writers because they've been around. They serve on the committees that award the prizes and fellowships. Their names are on the blurbs on the back covers of other people's books. You've heard some of them talking on the radio about other people's books.

You have a vague sense that you should ingratiate yourself to them, but you don't want to try beyond the bare social minimum. They aren't being very nice to you, and they're saying things you don't like about people you do like. People who were your mentors, old classmates who are now rising up into the public scene.

It's a strange world. This countrywide nexus of university and bar and bookstore and restaurant that lives always in the shadow of New York, which is where everyone claims they want to be.

None of it is what you thought it would be. There was a time when you had illusions. Fantasies of what it would be like to be a professor at a university. You'd walk the halls with all these other professors, all of them experts working on something interesting. Physicists, economists, anthropologists, historians. You'd ask about their work, and with enormous passion they'd tell you. Or fantasies of what it would be like to be a writer on a book tour. When you walked into the packed auditorium with a red scarf around your neck like Michael Douglas in *Wonder Boys*, everyone would have read every page. After all, that's why they came. To hear you talk about the book they read. To get it signed. To ask questions.

But that's not how it is. At the university, any university, almost no one who has achieved any sort of moneyed position wants to talk with you at a peer level about their work, and they probably don't really want you to talk to them about yours, even if they invited you to talk publicly about yours. If the subject does come up, it will be thirty seconds, forty max, before you'll out yourself as a person with an unorthodox idea. Or you'll express a more or less orthodox idea, but you'll say it wrong. It's a strange thing. In the hallways of any given university—gossip and resource-allocation politics aside—almost everyone who has achieved any sort of moneyed position seems to voice the same opinion about the same four or five subjects, and they seem to recite it using the same polysyllabic phrases as everyone else. A year later, this standard opinion might change. Or the four or five subjects of preoccupation might change. But if it does change, it changes for everyone at more or less the same time, and a new standard jargon comes along with it, which makes you feel like there's a conspiracy to hide from you the manual they're constantly revising and passing around.

At this bar, someone orders a couple of trays of hors d'oeuvres. You realize you haven't eaten since the early morning vending machine crackers. You've seen the grill menu, which includes wood-fired pizzas and hamburgers and breaded fish, but what arrives is a tray of tiny shrimp chips and tiny carrots with dipping sauce and paper-thin slices of salmon and cucumber on a cracker with no more surface area than one side of either of your thumbs.

The wood-fired pizza calls to you. When you ask the bartender how much it costs, the woman beside you waves him away. *No, no, no,* she says. *We got these to share.* She slides you one of the stingy plates, and a piece of the paper-thin salmon gets stuck between two back teeth.

New people arrive. The original people push tables together, and someone gives instruction about your new place to sit. One of the new people at your table is introduced as a Faulkner scholar. You try to start a conversation about the 1927 flood of the Mississippi River in the "Old Man" sections of Faulkner's *If I Forget Thee, Jerusalem*. But you're getting it wrong, and this guy wants to make sure you know. The woman sitting next to him says she knows *If I Forget Thee, Jerusalem* pretty well, but she likes your version better.

This is a kindness.

At the hotel you sleep on six-hundred-thread-count sheets. The room smells good. There is a drop of lavender on the pillow. Last night you were waiting in the cold for the knock on the door from the cop or the carjacker. Tonight there's a thermostat, a television, a sink, a shower, a room service menu.

Before you can make use of these amenities, you fall asleep. You're awakened by an alert on your phone. A message from a man who used to be your teacher. His wife is dying of leukemia in New Mexico. He doesn't yet know that he is, too. *Bad news, amigo,* the message says. *She's in hospice now. Today or tomorrow. After which, I am going to run away for a time, hoping that miles and miles from here I will know something wonderful about why we live.*

A woman takes you to breakfast. She has things to say, but the conversation stops cold every time you have things to say. Her eyes glaze over the same way eyes used to glaze over at parties in New York or Iowa City when someone asked where you lived and you said Toledo, Ohio. Or when someone asked what you were writing about and you said Southern Baptist missionaries in Haiti during the fall of the Duvalier regime.

It's not like you don't have anything interesting to say. Humankind is in your *ear* lately. Your social network is vast, and newly connected by the gossip channels of the internet. Plus, you're contemporary literature's token unmoneyed ex-fundamentalist semi-intellectual or whatever. The spy in the house of no commerce. Ugly things are always happening everywhere, but the further you get from the money, the more people will tell you the ugly truth about their lives. There is even sometimes a certain social currency to the ugly, and not just among the people without the money. You're afraid, sometimes, that in your quest to render the world you came from with unsparing veracity and great understanding, all you're really doing is ginning up a circus show for the amusement of some small segment of this opera and tiny sandwiches crowd.

Either way, circus material comes easy. Volunteers itself at least once a week. For example:

Last week in the Detroit airport, changing planes, you heard that a college classmate, a married music minister in Tennessee, has faked his own last dying words, claiming he was three breaths from his last in a Memphis hospital when he was really on a pay phone at the Hard Rock Cafe, as a way of breaking up with another woman to whom he had fraudulently become engaged.

You don't say things like these to this lady. At a certain point in the breakfast, she talks about the moment in her childhood—this happened at a dockside restaurant on the Chesapeake Bay, her father's sloop tied up five feet away—when she learned the proper way to hold the fork and the knife, and you realize she's talking about you. The way you're sawing through the powdered French toast and the charcuterie meats.

In a window-lit classroom in the afternoon, for an audience of three teachers and seven students, you read an Appalachian robot story loosely modeled on the Old Testament story Bob Dylan summarized as *God said Abraham kill me a son*. Usually you read for twenty minutes, but they've asked you to burn the hour, so you read the whole thing. When you're done, they clap tepidly. You sit for twenty minutes at a bookseller's signing table, but no one buys your book. Right in front of the bookseller, a man from the university hands you a check for three hundred dollars. You feel sorry for the bookseller as he packs up to leave with a box of your books and no money. So you give him fifteen dollars for your own book and figure it will only have cost you twelve dollars and seventy-five cents or so after the first royalties roll in.

Your flight touches down around one o'clock in the morning. You ride the shuttle to the long-term parking lot where you left your car. It's well lit, fenced in, patrolled, and therefore safe, so you sleep. At eight o'clock, when you leave the lot for the natatorium, you're sure to get a reimbursement receipt so the night's nine extra parking dollars are on somebody besides you.

On airplanes which are like other airplanes, you've been watching episodes of a TV show where a detective declares that *time is a flat circle*. That fact that today is another Wednesday following another Tuesday puts you in mind of a piece of language by the man whose wife is dying in New Mexico: *On Tuesday nothing, on*

Wednesday walls.

After you teach (*picnic, lightning*), you fly somewhere else to meet an audience. A small audience, usually, sometimes medium, occasionally quite large. If the audience is small, you feel bad. If the audience is big, you feel good. Sometimes you like the people a lot. When it is, you want to stay out late, see the city. Then you fly back Thursday night or Friday morning, weather the weekend somewhere in Indiana, maybe drive four hours to Toledo and see your kids. One of them looks into your eyes at bedtime and says: *Why are you always away?*

On the couch where you try to sleep, you think about something your wife said a few weeks earlier: *It's just an enormous amount of effort, but what's the return? All these years, all these miles on your body. Imagine if you had invested them in something easier when you had the chance. Something with reliable rewards, where the odds of success were greater. Law. Medicine. Neuroscience. Nuclear physics.*

There is a line of questioning implicit in the conversation: *What's wrong with you? Why do you keep doing this? What's so broken inside you that you need to keep chasing this? What is it you are looking for? Are you ever going to find it? Will there ever be a day when you decide it costs too much?*

You ponder the nature of *it*.

It hurts too much, so you push it away.

The next week, and the week after that, you do it all again.

There's a rhythm, a pattern.

Cold one night, absently pampered the next. You dread the pattern. It's wearing your body down. Totems become important. Comforts. Certain plastic cups. Certain fleece-lined shirts. Certain blankets. The natatorium shower is a good thing, but there's a part of you that wants to lie in a warm bath for three hours and read a book with your eyes half-open.

All over America you're looking for a bath.

It has to be the right tub. Clean, freshly cleaned, immaculately disinfected. For this reason you're leery of hotel bathtubs. As a child you saw a *20/20* expose on the shortcuts hotel housekeepers take in cleaning. Fungus on the countertops. Respiratory viruses on the phone. Fecal matter on every surface. The memory is worse now than the horror show you saw in real time, because you better understand the sum and substance of the proteins fluorescent on the sheets and walls under the swipe of the ultraviolet wand.

A tiny liberal arts college in the northeast puts you up in the guesthouse they built for visiting dignitaries, usually donors or trustees. The guesthouse bathtub is enormous. It has temperature controls and bubble jets. It looks clean. Anyway, you think you smell chlorine. All three hours in the water are good. Eyes half-open, you read a book you know almost by heart: *La Place de la Concorde Suisse*, by John McPhee, which has one of the better first sentences written in English in the twentieth century: *The Swiss have not fought a war for nearly five hundred years, and are determined to know how so as not to.*

Three hours later, a terrible stomach pain awakens you in the guesthouse. You rush, but you do not make it to the toilet in time. What you see when you wipe has colors and textures not made for Charmin. Blood, pus. There is a nauseating new smell—sweet rotting fish flesh sprayed by a skunk—and now begins the kind of gagging and vomiting jag at which your mother used to announce: *It's coming out both ends!*

It's hard to eat the diner food the next morning between trips to the restroom. The host asks how you liked the guesthouse. You say it's the best place you've stayed except the flagship Marriott in

Provo, Utah, which is the truth. He asks if you liked the tub. *Yes,* you say. *That's the tub I've been searching for.*

This is the second day in a row somebody has told me that, he says. *The night before you got here, one of our trustees stayed in the guesthouse and said the same thing. She needed it, too. She's been real sick. She had a surgery go badly. She just got out of the hospital. If you look at her face, she's still kind of green. But she loved that tub.*

The flight out is miserable. The waiting for the flight is miserable. The days, weeks, months ahead are miserable. No toilet is close enough. The sweet rot clings to you faintly. The smell never quite goes away. Your stomach punishes you for every ounce you take in. There's no sleeping in the car for a while. No way. At an extended stay you rent a room that smells like wet dog. Itinerant laborers arrive all night in bucket trucks and shine their headlights through room curtains that will only three-quarters close. You're not sleeping anyway. In bed you address yourself in the second person. *You can get through this, mudbutt. You can outlast it. You can win.* All night you lie as still as you are able. It's cold in the room, but you can't stop sweating. Your kidneys hurt. Your belly swells. You achieve a new state of consciousness somewhere between half sleep and waking death. You're forced to cancel a couple of readings. You make it to campus to meet your classes, but only barely.

At the walk-in clinic, a physician's assistant gives you a plastic cup and asks you to poop in it. She is seven months pregnant. She gives you a prescription for some pills. She takes your hand in hers and rests it on her belly so you can feel the baby kick before you perform the shameful act.

You're in Texas when she calls you with the news. Your large intestine is infested with a colony of bacteria called *C. difficile.* It's very dangerous. People die. It is imperative you take every one of those pills. It's weird you have it, though, because it's usually old people. In hospitals. In nursing homes. Have you shared intimate spaces with anyone who has recently convalesced in a nursing home or a hospital? A bed? A bathroom?

You're in New Hampshire when she calls for the first time with no news at all. *Hey,* she says, *I'm just calling to check on you. Are you seeing any change in your symptoms? I'm worried about you.* She calls again in South Carolina, Chicago, Los Angeles, San Diego. She doesn't call when you're in Seattle, at the biggest writer's conference in the world, where your publisher rents the historic Pike Place Market and throws you an enormous nighttime party. Music, lights, dancing. Looking out at the crowd, you see people you've always wanted to meet. Legends, heroes. They come to you, they shake your hand, you excuse yourself and race to destroy the men's room.

You're doing an interview at a radio station in Portland when you realize she's stopped calling, and you know what it means. She's delivered the baby. You wonder if you should call with congratulations. Ask how she's doing, how the baby's doing. Send a gift. You miss her. You have the sense that whatever protocol guides exchanges like these, it was long ago obliterated.

This was a kindness.

A friend says the best reciprocation of her kindness, now, would be to leave the physician's assistant alone. You see that this is true, so this is what you do.

It takes three rounds, but the pills kick in.

Your sickness is abating.

But I have come to believe that wasn't your only sickness.

III.

The seventh sailor was the last to leave port.

Donald Crowhurst was his name.

The year he turned sixteen, his father dropped dead of coronary thrombosis while gardening. All the family's money was in an Indian sports goods factory, which burned to the ground the same year, during the Partition riots.

Poverty followed.

While his mother scrounged loans from relatives, Crowhurst escaped into a party life in the Royal Air Force. Drinking beer, racing cars, sniffing mothballs. One night, he convinced a party of plastered officers to paint a telephone box yellow. Another, he waited until everyone was asleep and ran a motorcycle through the barracks.

This might have been why he was asked to leave the Royal Air Force the first time. The second time, he was caught trying to hot-wire a car to flee the city of Reading after crashing his own car into a bus.

By the time Crowhurst entered the race for the Golden Globe, he had been rejected from Cambridge (for failing his Latin exam), worked as a laboratory assistant, an electronics salesman, and a design engineer, got married, fathered four children, promoted his theory of the independence of the mind from the body, crashed two more cars, studied black magic, saved his mother from an attempted suicide, won election as councilman in the Bridgwater Central Ward, started a low-to-the-ground consumer electronics business, and kept it afloat by constant begging from investors and borrowing from banks.

In retrospect, Crowhurst had no business entering the race. He had never sailed farther than the weekend would allow. He chose to sail a kind of yacht he'd never sailed before, a trimaran, and he believed he could build a better kind of trimaran than any he could purchase. He had no money, but he convinced one of the loan-holders for his failing business that his best chance at repayment was to lend a little more, help him build the winning boat, with the company as collateral. It was a big bet, made by a man who was already maximally leveraged. If he lost the race, Crowhurst's young family, like his family of origin, would lose everything, including their home.

Things went wrong in the boatbuilding. A planned central computer was never completed. A topmast buoyancy bag was never installed. Self-steering screws were improperly secured. On a practice run in the English Channel with a local sailor, they unscrewed themselves from vibration any time the yacht's speed reached twelve knots.

Crowhurst gave a friend a set of sealed envelopes—a will and five goodbye letters—to be delivered to his wife and children in the event of his death. The friend promptly lost the envelopes, but a first draft of the letter to his wife was later found in his desk:

> I am going because it is worthwhile, it is my particular challenge, it will most likely bring benefits, but that is not why—I am going because I would have no peace if I stayed. Peace within myself, for no matter how happy a man is made by his wife and family life, if he turns down the one major challenge of his life he can never be the same, especially when the challenge is of his own devising! I am going because I must. I cannot turn away, nor do I wish to. I would certainly not go if I thought there was a very little chance of success, but I must go because I know I have a very, very good chance of success.

The boat began to fail as soon as he left port. He could only push the yacht to half the speed he'd planned. When he did, the screws came loose again, and he realized he'd brought no spares. Hull compartments began to leak. Because his bilge pumps were incorrectly piped, he had to bail them with a bucket. Saltwater flooded his generator, leaving him for a long while without power. All of this in the relative calm of the Atlantic. He realized the rougher waters of the Southern Ocean would break the boat apart.

Turning back was not an option. So he began to craft an elaborate lie.

Five weeks into his voyage, he created a false log, using faraway radio forecasts to describe weather he'd never seen in places he'd never been. A week later, he radioed a press release saying he'd sailed 243 miles in twenty-four hours, setting a new world record for a solo sailor.

His plan was to hang out in the South Atlantic while the other sailors circled the world, then reenter the race at the end. For three months he shut down his radio entirely. Because of his position at the time of the shutdown, newspapers deemed him the favorite to win the race. When his hull began to disintegrate, he stopped for repairs in a remote port in Argentina. Since no one reported the stop, he was not disqualified.

In April 1969, near Buenos Aires, he radioed to say that he was rounding the southern tip of South America. By then, Moitessier had already quit the race. The eventual winner, Robin Knox-Johnston, was close to the finish line, and the only other surviving entry, Nigel Tetley's, was on track to win a lesser prize, for speed.

Crowhurst believed that by winning neither prize, he'd avoid the scrutiny his logbooks could not bear. Perhaps, because of his fame at finishing the race few others could finish, he could rework his agreements, talk his lenders into another loan, sell a staggering amount of electronics on his new fame, save his business. But Tetley, alarmed by the news that Crowhurst was on his tail, pushed his yacht so hard that it broke apart near the Azores. When Tetley abandoned ship in an inflatable life raft, Crowhurst saw an ugly future before him.

In his last week of life, he began a new logbook, titled "Philosophy," in which he seemed to be writing himself toward suicide.

In seven days, he wrote twenty-five thousand words. He began with a critique of Einstein's *Relativity*, but then found something else in Einstein: When the math led Einstein to an impasse, Einstein "stipulated of his own free will" that the impasse go away.

Einstein—like Crowhurst—must have been a special man, a kind of prophet-seer whose mind could transcend the constraints of the body, of physics.

Crowhurst's "Philosophy" teemed with overcoming visions. The square root of minus one. A new kind of imaginary number as a portal to *extra physical existence*. Hysterical laughter and the plight of Black Americans. Mathematics as the language of god. A dark tunnel toward *cosmic integration*. A great leap, the mind from the body and into abstract existence. The possibility of becoming divine.

Against these visions, the dream of the race—in Crowhurst's words, *cosmic chess against the Devil*, or *the game*—faded, but the fear of facing the audience he had promised big things but failed to deliver never left him. They would *know*. This feeling may have been exacerbated by a cable from his publicist, which reached him not long before his death:

> BBC AND EXPRESS MEETING YOU WITH CLARE AND ME OFF SCILLIES YOUR TRIUMPH BRINGING ONE HUNDRED THOUSAND

> FOLK TEIGNMOUTH WHERE FUND NOW REACHING FIFTEEN HUNDRED PLUS MANY OTHER BENEFITS PLEASE GIVE ME SECRETS OF TRIP NEAR DEATH AND ALL THAT FOR PRE-PRESS SELLING OPPORTUNITIES MONEY OUTLOOK GOOD REPLY URGENT THINKING ABOUT ADVERTISING

Among the final words of his "Philosophy," Crowhurst wrote:

> Now is revealed the true nature and purpose and power of the game offence **I** am **I** am what **I** am and **I** see the nature of my offence . . . It is finished - It is finished - IT IS THE MERCY . . . **I** have not need to prolong the game It has been a good game that must be ended at the **I** will play this game when **I** choose **I** will resign the game . . .

Ten days later, his yacht was found adrift and unoccupied. Almost certainly he jumped overboard and drowned.

> **I, I, I, I, I, I, I, I . . .**

The impasse could not be stipulated away. They would *know*.

IV.

There is a sickness latent in the I. Parades of the self, such as solo races around the world or publicity tours, exacerbate it, but the sickness is ever-present. In history, in literature, in the people around us. All the heroes and antiheroes carried it. Even the people no one seemed to notice. The medium people Henry James called the *ficelles*. They carried it because we all carry it.

Notice me. Love me. Need me. See me. Hear me. Watch me win. Let me know I'm the most special.

The song of Need.

Need waiting to be beautifully met by another. Need acknowledged and unacknowledged by the one who carries it. Need in want of some measure of control. Urgent need. Distorting need. Need capable of enormous acts of sensuous expression, creative abundance, self-deception. Need capable of great destruction.

It is there in Walt Whitman:

I celebrate myself, and sing myself, and what I assume you shall assume, for every atom belonging to me as good belongs to you.

In Barry Hannah:

Sick soldier at your door. Now I come to Oxford and I am war.

In Mary Gaitskill:

I carry love wrapped in pain. That is my treasure and soon it will be yours.

In Denis Johnson:

Talk into my bullet hole. Tell me I'm fine.

*

The book you are right now reading—*How to Disappear and Why*—was once the manuscript I am still self-defeatingly withholding from my publisher in this unpleasant moment that will become the past.

Typing and deleting, typing and deleting.

Four times now, in four versions, it has been completed.

It is embarrassing to report that my right hand is shaking. For months the manuscript has existed in a form so nearly like the one you're reading that almost no one else could see daylight between the iterations. My finger hovers over the send button. There is nothing new that further fiddling with the sentences can accomplish. My delay in delivery brings to others an extraordinary inconvenience. Time is passing.

If I do not send it today, you might not see it at all.

Yet even today, at the end of things, I cannot let this manuscript go. They will see it in all its frailty and then they will see through it, to the author's frailty. They will know.

A little more time to revise, please. A few more days. A few more hours.

*

I'm thinking about the shame Donald Crowhurst must have felt on his last day on earth.

He must have imagined thousands of eyes on him.

To enter a race—

to climb a stage, to stand in front of a camera, to found a laboratory, to start a business, to fund a nonprofit, to start a war, to write a book . . .

—is to an enact a wish.

It is easy to deceive oneself about the nature of the wish one wants to fulfill.

*

I'm thinking about the myth of Moitessier, a myth that has seduced me for ten years.

Bernard Moitessier, the sailor who quit the race because he simply wanted to sail the seas.

Like all myths, it has been conveniently made.

Maybe Moitessier *was* so overcome by the life of the sea that the race no longer meant anything to him. Maybe Moitessier's plan all along was to quit the race in service to the romantic myth of his own making. Maybe he did plan to race hard to the finish, but he abandoned his plan at a moment of insecurity about the speed of the yachts behind him.

No one but Moitessier can know.

And yet the song Moitessier sang was a beautiful song. The race is not the thing. The present is the thing. The wind, the rain, the sea.

The underwater putty knife scraping the gooseneck barnacles from the hull bottom is the thing. Tasmania. The feeding habits of sharks. The porpoises of the South Pacific and the penguins of Galápagos. Fish soup the color of blood, the color of life, the color of the sunset past the Cape of Good Hope is the thing.

The myth is instructive.

I want to learn to separate the singer from the song.

*

~~*Bernard Moitessier, the sailor who quit the race because he simply wanted to sail the seas.*~~

~~*Bernard Moitessier, the sailor who quit the race because he had nothing left to say.*~~

Bernard Moitessier, who had something to say because he quit trying to win. Bernard Moitessier, who brought back the report about the things outside himself he sought and found.

*

Before he died, I went to visit my old teacher in New Mexico. He was seventy years old, gaunt, sitting on his stoop. I had never seen him look frail before. When I pulled up the dirt drive, he said: *See this stoop? I used to sit here with my wife. Then my wife died and I sat here with my dog. Now my dog is dead, so I sit here alone. I'm glad for your company.*

His eyes were beginning to fail him at night. He asked me to drive him around. He showed me the place where his elderly neighbor, a famous actor and stuntman, had gruesomely failed to complete a suicide attempt at the back of his property. He showed me the circular stone fort where the Spanish sheltered against Apache raids in the 1850s. He took me inside the nineteenth-century Catholic mission where he had presided over his son's marriage ceremony. He had the key to the courthouse jail cell where Billy the Kid freed his legs from irons with an axe, killed his captors, and rode one of their horses out of town singing.

As soon as we returned home, he got out the whiskey. *All I want to do is drink and bullshit,* he said. He'd read a biography of Raymond Carver. He was sour on it. The way Carver neglected his children, abused and discarded his first wife, cowardly prostrated himself before his editor Gordon Lish. Wasted his life.

He kept pouring, and I kept pace as best I could, but I'm no drinker. Five drinks in, I asked a question I'd been too sober to ask all the twenty years I'd known him: *Why did you stop writing?* He said he'd asked the same question of one his own teachers, another man who had stopped writing prematurely.

About that his old teacher had a theory:

Eventually all people of wisdom reach a moment of life in which they are satisfied with having nothing left to say.

But for me that wasn't it, he said. *I had reached a moment of life in which I was satisfied that I had said what I had to say. But I have a few regrets.*

He talked about the personal early stories he was most glad to have written. Versions of himself, realized in life or not. Fathers and sons. Men newly divorced. Golf course drinker-adulterers. Hobbled ex-athletes. The police station turned into a Bob's Big Boy restaurant.

He told me: *It wasn't until the end that I stopped singing the song of myself,* he said. *I got interested in the public story.* I'd read these stories. They were some of his best. The inquiry into a daughter's presumed kidnapping. The question of the Roswell aliens beneath the floorboards. The omniscient meditation on the shootings at Columbine High. *But by then there wasn't much left in the tank.*

He raised the glass as if to apologize. Swirled the whiskey at the bottom.

New Mexico is a long way from Indiana, amigo, he said. *Why is it you're here?*

The whole time we were staring at his bookshelf, and somewhere near the middle I saw the gray paperback spine that bore my name in white. *Did you read it?* I did not say. *Did you think it was good?*

V.

I am beginning to see that every expressive pursuit must hazard a landscape full of traps:

To do it for others.

To do it for the approval of others.

To do it for the applause of others.

To do it because it is urgent to be heard by others.

To do it to be proven right.

To do it to justify one's own bad choices.

To do it for riches.

To do it to get laid.

To do it to win.

To do it to cover your failure to win.

The satisfaction is always just beyond reach.

People will die for the lack of it. Crowhurst did. People will die *for* it. The monstrous James Dean fantasy: *Live fast, die young, and leave behind a good-looking corpse.*

People will die trying.

People risk their lives all the time. For riches, for fame. By air, by land, by sea. In smoky nightclubs. On football fields, in boxing rings, in hockey rinks.

I have risked my life for less.

How lucky that I never fell asleep on the interstate, got knifed to death in my sleep by a carjacker, breathed a fatal dose of carbon monoxide despite the cracked sunroof, succumbed to *C. difficile* in a dirty room, froze to death in the front seat.

*

To look only within is to see incompletely.

To demand—without reciprocating—the attention of others is a road to destruction.

To require adulation is to dance with death.

Look around.

At the edges of cities rich with grandmothers, armies are mobilizing. On the corner of 38th Street and Meridian, a man is playing a saxophone. In the backyard, in the poles and the tropics, in every ocean and sea, there is new and frightening weather. Rivers are jumping their banks. People are fleeing over borders. The world is filling with children.

*

There is a time to sing the song of oneself, but that time is not forever.

There are other songs.

The song of nature. The song of healing. The song of progress. The song of the ecstatic. The song of myth. The song of history.

In the voice of every singer you can hear the sickness, but not in every song.

All this time I've been wishing the wrong wish, but it's not too late.

For the song to grow the self must recede.

I see a path forward.

NOTES, SOURCES, AND SUGGESTIONS FOR FURTHER READING

HOW TO DISAPPEAR AND WHY

A partial list of additional sources:

Silence by Shūsaku Endō (translated by William Johnston in 1969, reprinted in 2016 by Picador)

The Box Man by Kōbō Abe (translated by E. Dale Saunders in 1974, reprinted in 2001 by Vintage)

Invisible Man by Ralph Ellison (Random House, 1952)

The House of Breath by William Goyen (fiftieth anniversary edition, TriQuarterly Books/Northwestern University Press, 1999)

"Ecstatic in the Poison" by Andrew Hudgins from *Ecstatic in the Poison* (Overlook Press, 2003)

the ghost comes with me by Letitia Trent (Ghost City Press, 2019)

In the Aeroplane Over the Sea by Neutral Milk Hotel (Merge Records, 1998)

The Naomi Poems: Book One: Corpse and Beans by Saint Geraud (Big Table/Follett, 1968)

A Manual for Cleaning Women by Lucia Berlin (Farrar, Straus and Giroux, 2015)

View with a Grain of Sand, Selected Poems by Wisława Szymborska (translated by Stanisław Barańczak and Clare Cavanagh, Harcourt, 1995)

Selected Stories of Alice Munro by Alice Munro (Alfred A. Knopf, 1996)

Unplugged by Neil Young (Reprise Records, 1993)

A THEORY OF GHOSTS

While I was circling this material, a retired firefighter, a man who used to take me to baseball games when I was a child, called me from a nursing home, using a technology called Facebook Messenger which will probably be obsolete and forgotten by the time you read this note. He hadn't seen anyone for a long time except for his roommate and the overworked nurses, he said, because of the COVID-19 quarantine. He was passing the time by reading the Bible on his phone, listening to audiobooks about baseball on his phone, and watching baseball on his phone. He was a large, tall man, 6'6", and he said his feet were rotting into the far end of his bed, because nursing home beds aren't made to fit giants. He told me about his love for his daughters and his continuing devotion to his wife, who had died of cancer some years earlier. While we talked, his roommate, who suffered from dementia and could not support any weight on his feet, fell out of his bed, not for the first time, and for the fifteen minutes it took to get someone to help the man back into the bed, the man lay on the floor and screamed. We didn't talk for all those fifteen minutes, because my friend spent all of them trying with great gentleness to comfort his roommate with words. *It's OK, buddy. I called the nurse. She's on the way. They're gonna take good care of you. You don't remember, but we've been here before, and it always turns out OK. When this is over, we're gonna watch baseball and eat vanilla pudding. We're gonna drink water the way you like it, with the ice cubes in it. We're gonna call your sister. Hang tight, brother. We're gonna get through this together.*

After the screaming was over, my friend apologized for the interruption. He said he'd reached out because he was remembering knowing me as a child, and he wanted to say some encouraging words to the adult I had become. He said he was very lonely, he'd enjoyed our call, and if I had an extra minute, would I call him again?

A few days later, he died. When I searched the internet for his obituary, I also found newspaper stories, TV reports, and so on. Mostly, they were stories about his generosity. I heard more of these stories when I called other people I knew who knew him better than I did, who had stayed in his life in the forty or so years I hadn't. The fireman who helped when there wasn't enough food in the house. The fireman who topped off the missing tuition money. The fireman who quietly paid the missing month of rent, so the family wouldn't get evicted. The fireman who heard a migrant family didn't have a car, so he quietly bought them one.

I write this here so he will be remembered by anyone who might read this note. Pierre Czernowski was his name.

A partial list of additional sources:

"The Snake Doctors" by Frank Stanford from *What About This: Collected Poems of Frank Stanford* (Copper Canyon Press, 2015)

As a Friend by Forrest Gander (New Directions, 2008)

Interview with the Vampire by Anne Rice (Alfred A. Knopf, 1976)

THE UBER DIARIES

An earlier version of this essay originally appeared in *New Ohio Review*. For a while I flirted with turning it into a novel. Around this time, my seventy-year-old uncle pled guilty to one count of mail fraud as part of an embezzlement scheme in which he stole between $1.6 and 5.8 million from the pension fund for a charity formerly known, in the time of polio, as the Crippled Children's Society. It was hard to keep that out of the novel, but after I put it in, I realized it wasn't something I could publish, because I didn't want my writing to alienate my family of origin, as it had in the past. I don't believe anymore that literary art—or any kind of art—is worth that kind of disruption to love, which is the scarcest commodity in the world. So I quashed the novel, and felt great relief in the quashing. There are two three-hundred-page drafts on a hard drive in Indianapolis. They sit alongside unpublished and abandoned partial or completed drafts of six regular-length novels, three collections of short stories, eighteen screenplays, one draft of a book-length essay about competitive card playing and the attempted flooding of Anderson, Indiana, and one 1,200-page monstrosity about the sexual lives of three generations of Baptist missionaries in the mountains of Ouest Province, in Haiti.

Selah.

A partial list of additional sources:

"Narcissus and Echo" by Fred Chappell from *Spring Garden: New and Selected Poems* (Louisiana State University Press, 1995)

Regarding the Pain of Others by Susan Sontag (Penguin, 2003)

ON THE DESIRE TO REJECT NARCISSISM

This essay's presiding spirit is Lydia Davis.

A partial list of additional sources:

"Lose Yourself" by Eminem from *8 Mile* (Interscope Records, 2002)

"Alexander Hamilton" and "My Shot" by Lin-Manuel Miranda from *Hamilton: An American Musical* (Atlantic Records, 2015)

"The Only Animal" by Franz Wright from *Walking to Martha's Vinyard* (Alfred A. Knopf, 2003)

"Why I Am Not a Buddhist" by Molly Peacock from *Cornucopia: New and Selected Poems* (W. W. Norton, 2003)

Never Drank the Kool-Aid by Touré (Picador, 2006)

"Ten Year Town" by Hailey Whitters from *The Dream* (Pigasus Records, 2020)

"Argentina" by Tony Hoagland from *What Narcissism Means to Me* (Graywolf, 2003)

"The Beforelife: Franz Wright" by Alice Quinn from *The New Yorker*, July 1, 2001

Freud: The Mind of the Moralist by Philip Rieff (Viking, 1959)

THE LIZARD, THE STINK, THE BEAR, THE GAME, THE ROAD TO SOMEWHERE

A partial list of additional sources:

The House of the Dead: Siberian Exile Under the Tsars by Daniel Beer (Alfred A. Knopf, 2016)

The Book of Laughter and Forgetting by Milan Kundera (translated by Aaron Asher, HarperCollins, 1996)

One Day in the Life of Ivan Denisovich by Aleksandr Solzhenitsyn (translated by H. T. Willetts, Farrar, Straus and Giroux, 1991)

The Gulag Archipelago by Aleksandr Solzhenitsyn (three volumes, originally published 1974, reprinted in 2007 by HarperCollins)

The Dew Breaker by Edwidge Danticat (Alfred A. Knopf, 2004)

Dalton Trumbo by Bruce Cook (Charles Scribner's Sons, 1977)

Black Lamb and Grey Falcon by Rebecca West (originally published 1941–1943, reprinted in 2007 by Penguin Books)

I Am a Japanese Writer by Dany Laferriere (translated by David Homel, Douglas & McIntyre, 2011)

Clockers by Richard Price (Houghton Mifflin, 1992)

"What We Talk About When We Talk About Anne Frank" by Nathan Englander, from *What We Talk About When We Talk About Anne Frank*, Alfred A. Knopf, 2012)

Gary Saul Morson's *New York Review of Books* essays on Russian literature and Soviet metaphor (various issues, 2016–2023)

René Girard in general, but a good place to start is *The Girard Reader*, edited by James G. Williams (reprinted in 1996 by Crossroad)

The Dawn Watch by Maya Jasanoff (Penguin, 2020)

Pooh's Heffalump Movie (DisneyToon Studios, 2005)

HIDING IN PLAIN SIGHT

This meditation was prompted by a summer of work, in collaboration with Blake Kimzey, on a screenplay adaptation of Phillip H. McMath's 2015 stage play *Karski's Message*. I hope that one day soon that movie, or another like it, will see the green light, because there are few stories more necessary to our historical moment than Jan Karski's.

The most authoritative Karski source is E. Thomas Wood and Stanislaw M. Jankowski's historical biography *Karski: How One Man Tried to Stop the Holocaust* (John Wiley & Sons, 1994). It is the source upon which my essay is most dependent. But the place to start, for those interested in learning more, is *Karski and the Lords of Humanity* (Apple Film Productions, 2015), a documentary film by Slawomir Grunberg, which includes, in addition to important contextualizing contributions by E. Thomas Wood, outtakes from Karski's interviews with Claude Lanzmann which were not included in *Shoah*, his landmark nine-hour documentary on the Holocaust.

A partial list of additional sources:

Story of a Secret State, a memoir with fictionalized passages in deference to the exigencies of the ongoing world war, by Jan Karski (Houghton Mifflin, 1944)

Shoah, a documentary film by Claude Lanzmann (New Yorker Films, 1985)

The Karski Report (Le Rapport Karski), a forty-eight-minute "extended interview" with Karski that expands upon and amplifies his testimony from *Shoah*, by Claude Lanzmann (ARTE, 2010)

The Patagonian Hare by Claude Lanzmann (translated by Frank Wynne, Farrar, Straus and Giroux, 2012)

Special Operations Executive Manual: How to Be an Agent in Occupied Europe (HarperCollins, 2014)

S.O.E. in France by M. R. D. Foot (Her Majesty's Stationery Office, 1966)

S.O.E.: The Scientific Secrets by Fredric Boyce and Douglas Everett (Sutton, 2003)

Adaptive Coloration in Animals by Hugh B. Cott (Methuen & Company, 1940)

JUNK TEMPLES

Because of the nature of this essay, a complete list of sources would be longer than this appendix, beginning with J. F. Turner's *Howard Finster: Man of Visions* (Alfred A. Knopf, 1989), Lawrence Weschler's *Vermeer in Bosnia* (Pantheon, 2004) and *Everything That Rises: A Book of Convergences* (McSweeney's, 2006), and John M.

MacGregor's *Henry Darger: In the Realms of the Unreal* ([Delano Greenidge Editions, 2002] which, fair warning, takes a darker view of Darger than later observers would). But here's a suggestion, for starters: Go to the library, the internet, wherever it is that people find their documentary films in the part of the future when you're reading this book, and get caught up on some of the greats among junk temple erectors: Jean-Michel Basquiat (Tamra Davis's *Jean-Michel Basquiat: The Radiant Child* [2010] is the place to start), Francis Ford Coppola, Joan Didion, Muhammad Ali, Darger, etc. They all speak to each other, and one will lead to another. Pretty soon you'll be reading the conversations between Toni Morrison and William Faulkner, Philip Roth and John Updike, William Shakespeare and Ngũgĩ wa Thiong'o, Ralph Ellison and Saul Bellow, William Trevor and Yiyun Li, etc. You'll be hearing the Kim Deal in your Kurt Cobain and the extraordinary presence of the Russian-born lexicographer Nicolas Slonimsky's *Thesaurus of Scales and Melodic Patterns* (Charles Scribner's Sons, 1947) in John Coltrane's "sheets of sound." Also: Joyelle McSweeney's *The Necropastoral* (University of Michigan Press, 2015), Johannes Göransson's *entrance to a colonial pageant in which we all begin to intricate* (Tarpaulin Sky Press, 2011), Terrance Hayes's *Who are the Tribes* (Pilot Books, 2011), the Book of Ecclesiastes (and Mark Jarman's poem "Questions for Ecclesiastes" [*Questions for Ecclesiastes*, Story Line Press, 1997]), Kenzaburō Ōe's *Seventeen and J* (Blue Moon Books, 1996), Kirstin Valdez Quade's *The Five Wounds* (W. W. Norton, 2021), Abraham Smith's *Hank* (Action Books, 2010), Nana Nkweti's *Walking on Cowrie Shells* (Indigo Press, 2021), Samuel Beckett's *The Lost Ones* (Grove, 1972), Mary Ruefle's *Madness, Rack, and Honey* (Wave Books, 2012), Edwidge Danticat's *The Dew Breaker* (Alfred A. Knopf, 2004), Maurice Manning's *Lawrence Booth's Book of Visions* (Yale University

Press, 2001), *Blue Nights* by Joan Didion (Vintage, 2012), *On Being Blue* by William Gass (NYRB Classics 2014), *Bluets* by Maggie Nelson (Wave Books, 2009), *A Thousand Plateaus* by Gilles Deleuze and Felix Guattari (translated by Brian Massumi, University of Minnesota Press, 1987), *Autobiographical Essays, Notebooks, Evocations, Interviews* by William Goyen (University of Texas Press, 2007), Sappho's "Fragment 105(a)," translated by Anita George (in *Poetry*, June 1994), "To the Writers of *The Unit*" by David Mamet (an unpublished letter widely circulated on the internet), "The Rules" by Lee K. Abbott (unpublished handout, c. 1995), *Petty: The Biography* by Warren Zanes (St. Martin's Griffin, 2015), *Fires* by Raymond Carver (Vintage/Ebury, 1985), *The Waste Land* by T. S. Eliot (Boni & Liveright, 1922), *Selected Poems of Robert Creeley* by Robert Creeley (University of California Press, 1991), *The Lonely City* by Olivia Laing (Picador, 2017), *Collected Poems* by Jane Kenyon (Graywolf, 2005), *The Collected Poems of W. B. Yeats* by W. B. Yeats (Macmillan, 1989), *The Collected Poems of James Laughlin* by James Laughlin (New Directions, 2014), *Map: Collected and Last Poems* by Wisława Szymborska (edited by Clare Cavanagh, HarperCollins, 2015), *Bringing the Shovel Down* by Ross Gay (University of Pittsburgh Press, 2011), Jane Smiley's author interview with Robert Birnbaum for *Identity Theory* (online, June 18, 2003), and *Runaway: New Poems* by Jorie Graham (Ecco, 2020). It doesn't matter how you go about it, or which temples you do or don't decide to visit, or how long you stay there, or if you are or aren't inspired to build a temple or temples of your own, because it's easy to admit that, against the vast backdrop of time and the universe, nothing matters. But the better choice is to proceed as if it does matter, more than anything it matters, and in another way of thinking it really does, because this is the life and the time you have.

This essay's presiding spirits are Maggie Nelson and Jonathan Lethem.

THE SICKNESS AND THE SONG

In the sections concerning the race for the Golden Globe, I have tried to strictly harmonize the places and dates with the historical record. In the memory-derived second section, portions of the events chronology of the book tour have been altered or reordered, and place names and characters have been disguised or composited. This choice is intended as a concession to decency, in order to protect the identities of other people who didn't ask to be part of this book.

A partial list of sources:

Foggy and sometimes contradictory memories of the road, the sky, the bar, the car, the plane, the natatorium

The Long Way by Bernard Moitessier (Doubleday, 1975)

The Strange Last Voyage of Donald Crowhurst by Nicholas Tomalin and Ron Hall (Hodder & Stoughton, 1970)

Off the Deep End: A History of Madness at Sea by Nic Compton (Bloomsbury, 2017)

A World of My Own by Robin Knox-Johnston (Morrow, 1970)

A Voyage for Madmen by Peter Nichols (HarperCollins, 2001)

The Longest Race by Hal Roth (W. W. Norton, 1983)

Deep Water, a documentary film by Jerry Rothwell and Louise Osmond (Pathé Productions, 2006)

"Cormac McCarthy's Venomous Fiction" by Richard B. Woodward (*New York Times*, April 19, 1992)

Hawaii by James Michener (Dial, 2002)

"The Nature and Aim of Fiction" by Flannery O'Connor (Farrar, Straus and Giroux, 1969)

"Highway 61 Revisited" by Bob Dylan from *Highway 61 Revisited* (Columbia Records, 1965)

True Detective by Nic Pizzolatto (HBO, 2014)

"On Tuesday Nothing, on Wednesday Walls" by Lee K. Abbott from *Wet Places at Noon* (University of Iowa Press, 1997)

Lolita by Vladimir Nabokov (Vintage, 1997)

La Place de la Concorde by John McPhee (Farrar, Straus and Giroux, 1984)

"Song of Myself" by Walt Whitman from *Leaves of Grass* (Philadelphia, 1892)

The Devil's Treasure by Mary Gaitskill (McNally Editions, 2023)

"Sick Soldier at Your Door" by Barry Hannah from *Long, Last, Happy* (Grove, 2010)

"Steady Hands at Seattle General" by Denis Johnson from *Jesus' Son* (Picador, 1992)

GHOST ESSAYS

The written essays in this book are intended to live among the unwritten essays on the subject of *How to Disappear and Why*. Some of these essays are suggested in the anaphora of the thirteen notions to investigate. Others live in the spaces between and around the personal essays that follow. Some are affirmations, parallel experiences, in-the-meantimes. Others are complications, disputes, or refutations. All are welcome, because to essay is to attempt, and all attempts fall short of the glory of the ghosts. Also welcome: further inquiries into the lizard, the scapegoat, the survivor in winter. Further elucidations of the ephemeral and the ecstatic.

Further explorations of the oceans beyond the tyranny of the I.

I hope it's understood that most if not all of these currently unwritten essays will not be nurtured into the light by the author of this book. If there was anything here for you, one great reciprocal honor you could bestow would be to nurture one or two of them into the light yourself. If you did, you'd be doing so with my encouragement and blessing, because I'd like to read them in magazines and literary journals and websites and a book bearing your name.

Literature is a conversation. It is a mistake to think you need an invitation.

A BROAD STREAM OF UNDERLYING GENERATIVE SOURCES YOU WOULDN'T KNOW WERE SIGNIFICANTLY IN THE DNA OF THIS BOOK UNLESS I TYPED THEM HERE

"The Apology" by Stephen Dixon from *Interstate* (Henry Holt, 1995)

Too Late by Stephen Dixon (Harper & Row, 1978)

"Gusev" by Anton Chekhov from *Forty Stories* (translated by Robert Payne, Penguin Random House, 1991)

"Lust" by Susan Minot from *Lust and Other Stories* (Houghton Mifflin, 1989)

"What Has That to Do with Me?" by Yiyun Li from *Gettysburg Review*, Summer 2003

"You Drive" by Christine Schutt from *Nightwork* (Alfred A. Knopf, 1996)

"The Solutions to Ben's Problem" by Bonnie Jo Campbell from *Diagram*, 7.4

"Eleven Beds" by William Harrison from *Texas Heat and Other Stories* (Texas Review Press, 2005)

How They Were Found by Matt Bell (Keyhole Press, 2010)

The Collectors by Matt Bell (Caketrain Press, 2009)

"Happy Endings" by Margaret Atwood from *Murder in the Dark* (Coach House Press, 1983)

"Against Specificity" by Douglas Watson from *The Era of Not Quite* (BOA Editions, 2013)

"Makedonija," by Miroslav Penkov from *East of the West:Stories* (Picador, 2012)

"Detroit Arcadia," by Rebecca Solnit from *Harper*'s, July 2007

"Vien a ca, Beda" by Bart Skarzynski from *Missouri Review*, Winter 2007

"The Bonus Hunter: Confessions of an Online Gambler" by Todd James Pierce from *Missouri Review*, Fall 2008

"What Reconciles Me to My Own Death" by John Berger from *Selected Essays of John Berger* (Vintage, 2003)

"All We Read Is Freaks" by William Bowers from *Oxford American*, January/February 2003

"Miroir Daniere," by Madison Smartt Bell from *The Hudson Review*, Vol XLVIII #4

"Magic: The Essay," by Mike Alber from *Hobart 9: Games*, October 2008

"Army" by Ben Folds from *The Unauthorized Biography of Reinhold Messner* (550 Music, 1999)

"Saints" by Kim Deal from *Last Splash* (4AD, 1993)

"Have You Seen Me Lately?" by Adam Duritz from *Recovering the Satellites* (DGC Records, 1996)

"[at last we killed the roaches]" by Lucille Clifton from *Good Woman: poems and a memoir 1969–1980* (BOA Editions, 1987)

"The Glass" by Sharon Olds from *The Father* (Alfred A. Knopf, 1992)

"The Pope's Penis" by Sharon Olds from *The Gold Cell* (Alfred A. Knopf, 1987)

"Brief Lives in California" by John L'Heureux from *Desires* (Holt, Rinehart and Winston, 1981)

"Final Proof of Fate and Circumstance" by Lee K. Abbott from *All Things, All at Once* (W. W. Norton, 2006)

"Goodbye, Little Saigon" by Tom Quach from *Bennington Review*, issue 11

"Love and Honor and Pity and Pride and Compassion and Sacrifice" by Nam Le from *The Boat* (Alfred A. Knopf, 2008)

Car Wheels on a Gravel Road by Lucinda Williams (Mercury Records, 1998)

Motif-Index of Folk Literature by Stith Thompson (six volumes, Indiana University Press, 1955–1958)

Silva Rhetoricae: The Forest of Rhetoric by Gideon Burton, https://rhetoric.byu.edu

The Poetics of Space by Gaston Bachelard (translated by Maria Jolas, Beacon Press, 1969)

Create Dangerously by Edwidge Danticat (Princeton University Press, 2010)

Maps and Legends by Michael Chabon (McSweeney's, 2008)

Wonderbook by Jeff VanderMeer (Abrams, 2018)

The Creative Act: A Way of Being by Rick Rubin (Penguin, 2023)

Skitter on Take-Off by Vic Chesnutt (Vapor Records, 2009)

The Disappointment Artist by Jonathan Lethem (Doubleday, 2005)

All Aunt Hagar's Children by Edward P. Jones (Amistad, 2006)

From Old Notebooks by Evan Lavender-Smith (Dzanc Books, 2013)

100 Essays I Don't Have Time to Write by Sarah Ruhl (Farrar, Straus and Giroux, 2014)

Dispatches by Michael Herr (Alfred A. Knopf, 1977)

A Mile Down by David Vann (Da Capo, 2005)

Big World by Mary Miller (Short Flight/Long Drive Books, 2009)

The Journals of John Cheever (Alfred A. Knopf, 1991)

Notes: On the Making of Apocalypse Now by Eleanor Coppola (Simon & Schuster, 1979)

The Faulkner-Cowley File edited by Malcolm Cowley (Viking, 1966)

Pitch Black by Renata Adler (1983, reprinted in 2013 by New York Review of Books Classics)

Stoner by John Williams (1965, reprinted in 2006 by New York Review of Books Classics)

And So We Die, Having First Slept by Jennifer Spiegel (Five Oaks Press, 2018)

In the Lake of the Woods by Tim O'Brien (Houghton Mifflin, 1995)

The Things They Carried by Tim O'Brien (Houghton Mifflin, 1990)

For the Relief of Unbearable Urges by Nathan Englander (Alfred A. Knopf, 1999)

The Puttermesser Papers by Cynthia Ozick (Alfred A. Knopf, 1997)

The Collected Stories of Isaac Babel (W. W. Norton, 2002)

The Collected Stories of Isaac Bashevis Singer (Farrar Straus & Giroux, 1982)

American Pastoral by Philip Roth (Houghton Mifflin, 1997)

Patrimony by Philip Roth (Simon & Schuster, 1991)

Deception by Philip Roth (Simon & Schuster, 1990)

Sabbath's Theater by Philip Roth (Houghton Mifflin, 1995)

50 transitional sentences from *We Tell Ourselves Stories in Order to Live* by Joan Didion (Alfred A. Knopf, 2006)

INTERLOCUTORS

These essays are enriched, in form, content, and style, by correspondence and conversations with other writers and artists, some predating the writing by a decade or more, with the following colleagues and friends, so much so that any acknowledgment of their efforts seems to belong more rightly alongside the sources than in the thank yous (and bear in mind that any and all shortcomings in the work belong only to the author, who doesn't always listen to good advice):

Douglas Watson (for the last twenty years my first reader and uncompensated line editor), Tom Quach (real true friend and traveling companion to Ground Zero), Phong Nguyen (the most generous of readers), David Wanczyk (the original and crucial editor for "The Uber Diaries," in *New Ohio Review*), Jamie Renda (the smartest and most challenging reader and Steinbeck/Plantagenet/Don scholar in America), Karen Kovacik (who I trust above all others concerning all things lyrical), Robert Rebein (narrative cowboy and A-1 bullshit detector), Dini Parayitam (constant encourager and sometime collaborator), Blake Kimzey (constant collaborator and sometime encourager), Gregory Cowles (the original editor of a review of Kirstin Valdez Quade's *Night at the Fiestas* in the *New York Times Book Review*, from which necessary language about Jaroslav Pelikan's *Jesus Through the Centuries* [Yale University Press, 1985] was culled), Donald Ray Pollock (who told me about William Goyen), Lawrence Weschler (who appeared briefly in my life, twice, and caused me to rethink my relationship to the intellectual work of reading, reporting, and writing), Sarah Elaine Smith and Joyelle McSweeney (who are likewise interested in secret doors, which Joyelle calls wounds and membranes and Sarah calls portals), Jennifer Percy (whose TK-and-metaphors method, learned late night in a basement in Iowa City, among pool tables and index cards and "beetles cooling themselves in the pee foam," was the drafting-and-building-up method of this book), Jason Gray (who taught me scansion, and who is always kind), Natalie Shapero (who taught us all what one does after the scansion is complete and it's time to move on to the bigger things), David Bowen (fellow traveler in life-altering grief), Kathleen Rooney (who helped me learn about what it means to operate as an adult), David Baker (who taught me how to read poetry), David Hoegberg (who showed me how the South African novelist Zoë Wicomb made point of view out of what her characters were reading), the late Jane Bradley (who taught me about "the girl with the big heart who wants two things"), the late John L'Heureux (who would have been memorialized at length in this book if there had been space for one more essay), David Daley and Andrew Sean Greer (who were willing to take a lot of time helping me think through Alice Munro), Karolina Waclawiak (who mailed me the magic stone), Garth Greenwell (who on the day of courage showed up big-time), Sara Harrell, Bart Skarzynski, Letitia Trent, Ed Falco, Shahnaz Habib, Mitchell L. H. Douglas, Sarah Layden, Terry Kirts, Hannah Haas, Jane Schultz, Frank Bill, Joey Franklin, Melissa Chadburn, Dara Kell, Maureen Traverse, Ed Fry, Meredith Blankenship, Kelly Abbott, Lisa Hendrickson, Andrew Weber, Rachel Dupont, Claire Christoff, Dan Barden, Christian TeBordo, Tim Horvath, Andrew Ervin, Phil Goff, Tom Davis, Laura Kopchick, Miroslav Penkov, Andrew Brininstool, Alice Elliott Dark, Justin Lee, Scott Kaukonen, Nana Nkweti, Elizabeth Coffman-Mackey, Nate Marquam, Jennifer Spiegel, Brian Jabas Smith, Nina MacLaughlin, Deb Olin Unferth, Kelly Smith, Neil Smith, Pamela Erens, James Yeh, Lincoln Michel, and Kelly Schoenegge (friends, readers, and encouragers), Kristen

Radtke and Kirby Gann (who, through hard work and tremendous intervention, made possible the living I now enjoy), Amelia Gray, Lee Shipman, Brian Evenson, and Nic Pizzolatto (who tried to help me when the world was closing down around me, in California and even after), Harry Thomason and Linda Bloodworth-Thomason (the most interesting people I've ever known, and friends for life), Mikal Wyatt, Jeff Garrison, Dave Scherer, Cheyanna Rodarmel, and Aaron Tarbell (who helped me with the Pokémon lore), Daniel, Laura, Ben, Steve, Joshuah, Sherman, Erin, Andrew, Blake, Kathy, Cal, Pinckney, Jeffrey, Ethan, and Lee (who helped me in various ways before it was briefly fashionable), Jon Saari (who read and discussed books with me and helped me learn to be a reader at the beginning of my career), Steve Gillis and Dan Wickett (important literary friends), James Yoder (soldier), Matt Bell (who is walking the same road but with greater speed and style), and Jake Sentgeorge (childhood frenemy, virtuoso pianist, high school quarterback, concert opera singer, poet, philosopher, important mid-life friend and confidant, in that chronological order).

THANK YOU

To my editor, Sarah Gorham, who took a chance on this book, and who stayed with me when the hardest things of life intervened, even though she claimed to have retired.

And to the team at Sarabande, especially Danika Isdahl, who is owed a medal (perhaps sainthood) for her patience with me. Also: Kristen Renee Miller (ditto), Joanna Englert, Sam Hall, and Natalie Wollenzien.

To my literary agent, Katherine Fausset.

To my family.

ACKNOWLEDGMENTS

Fred Chappell, "Narcissus and Echo" from *Spring Garden: New and Selected Poems*, Louisiana State University Press, 1995. Used with permission.

"The Only Animal" from WALKING TO MARTHA'S VINEYARD by Franz Wright, copyright © 2003 by Franz Wright. Used by permission of Alfred A. Knopf, an imprint of the Knopf Doubleday Publishing Group, a division of Penguin Random House LLC. All rights reserved.

"Why I Am Not A Buddhist". Copyright © 1995 by Molly Peacock, from CORNUCOPIA: NEW AND SELECTED POEMS by Molly Peacock. Used by permission of W. W. Norton & Company, Inc.

Tony Hoagland, "Argentina" from *What Narcissism Means to Me.* Copyright © 2003 by Tony Hoagland. Reprinted with the permission of The Permissions Company, LLC on behalf of Graywolf Press, Minneapolis, Minnesota, graywolfpress.org.

From "Dreams", from *Map: Collected and Last Poems by Wisława Szymborska*, Edited by Clare Cavanagh. Translated from the Polish by Clare Cavanagh and Stanislaw Baranczak. All works by Wisława Szymborska copyright (c) The Wisława Szymborska Foundation. English translation (c) 2015 by HarperCollins Publishers. Used by permission of HarperCollins Publishers.

Frank Stanford, "The Snake Doctors" from *What About This: Collected Poems of Frank Stanford*. Copyright © 2015 by Ginny Crouch Stanford and C. D. Wright, Estate of Frank Stanford. Reprinted with the permission of The Permissions Company, LLC on behalf of Copper Canyon Press, coppercanyonpress.org.

Robert Creeley, excerpt from "The Door" from *The Collected Poems of Robert Creeley 1945–1975*. Copyright © 1967 by Robert Creeley. Reprinted with the permission of The Permissions Company, LLC on behalf of the Estate of Robert Creeley.

Four lines of the title poem of Runaway by Jorie Graham. Copyright (c) 2020 by Jorie Graham. Used by permission of HarperCollins Publishers.

KYLE MINOR is the author of *Praying Drunk* (Sarabande, 2014), winner of the 2015 Story Prize Spotlight Award. His essays, stories, and novellas appear online and in print in *The Atlantic*, *Esquire*, *Iowa Review*, *Southern Review*, *Missouri Review*, *Best American Nonrequired Reading 2013*, *Best American Mystery Stories 2008* and *2015*, and the *New York Times Book Review*.

Sarabande Books is a nonprofit independent literary press headquartered in Louisville, Kentucky. Established in 1994 to champion poetry, fiction, and essay, we are committed to creating lasting editions that honor exceptional writing. With over two hundred titles in print, we have earned a dedicated readership and a national reputation as a publisher of diverse forms and innovative voices.